DISCOUNTS
& GOOD DEALS
FOR SENIORS IN TEXAS

Gulf Publishing Company
Houston, Texas

DISCOUNTS & GOOD DEALS
FOR SENIORS IN TEXAS

THE BEST BARGAINS AND DEALS FROM ABILENE TO ZAVALLA FOR AGES 50 AND UP

*This book was written as a gift for my parents,
Stanley and Ginger Spade. It is dedicated to them
and my grandmother, Ina Spade, who inspired
me to become a writer.*

DISCOUNTS & GOOD DEALS
FOR SENIORS IN TEXAS

Gulf Publishing Company
Book Division
P.O. Box 2608 □ Houston, Texas 77252-2608

10   9   8   7   6   5   4   3   2   1

Library of Congress Cataloging-in-Publication Data
Spade-Kershaw, Sylvia.
    Discounts & good deals for Texas Seniors : from Abilene
to Zavalla / Sylvia Spade-Kershaw.
        p.   cm.
    Includes index.
    ISBN 0-88415-181-6 (alk. paper)
    1. Shopping—Texas—Directories.   2. Discounts for the
aged—Texas—Directories.   I. Title.
TX336.5.T4S63   1997
380.1′45′00025764—dc21   97-20814
                                                 CIP

Contents

Please Note:

Texas continues to experience many telephone area code changes. We have attempted to correct these changes prior to reprinting this book; however, you may need to consult your local telephone company if you experience area code discrepancies.

Acknowledgments

I am fortunate to have some extraordinary people to thank for helping me write this book.

I owe thanks to everyone who contributed ideas, insights, and information for this book. Thanks to Gabrielle Descouzis, the staff of Family Eldercare in Austin, Paula Johnson at the State Department on Aging, Nancy Snead and Carole Barusch at the Texas state office of AARP, and my computer consultants, Larry Greenhaw and Ron Bass.

Much gratitude goes to Lynne Paulson and the staff of the Westbank Community Library for their tireless and creative energy in helping me with research. Without the creative suggestions of my editor, Joyce Alff, the manuscript would have been incomplete.

Finally my heartfelt thanks to my husband, Larry; daughter, Melissa; and my parents for their unwavering support and patience both for me and for this book.

Introduction

My parents are in their late sixties, an age I like to refer to as "chronologically gifted." Many of my friends and I are part of that boisterous bunch known as the baby boomers, and ready or not, the first wave in an ocean of boomers began turning 50 in 1996. By AARP's definition, they can now be considered senior citizens!

In its August 1996 "Golden Discounts for Silver Market" article, *The New York Times News Service* states that today, one in eight people is 65 or older and that in ten years, the 55-to-74-year-old group will account for almost 50 percent of the population. This group reportedly possesses half the country's discretionary spending power and 77 percent of its financial assets—not to mention the time to spend them. (Source: Pedersen, Laura, "Golden Discounts for Silver Market," *The New York Times News Service,* reprinted in the *Austin American-Statesman,* August 11, 1996)

Those statistics are just as true in Texas. According to 1994 Census figures provided by the Texas Department on Aging, there are more than 2.5 million people living in Texas who are 60 or older. As the baby boomers enter this "age of maturity," the buying potential of Texas seniors will increase exponentially, and the senior market will become an increasingly powerful market segment. In their book, *Segmenting the Mature Market,* Carol M. Morgan and Doran J. Levy, Ph.D., warn "Marketers who ignore the senior market today will have a difficult time getting a foothold serving the needs of aging boomers. Planning now is essential." (Source: Morgan, Carol M. and Levy, Ph.D., Doran J., *Segmenting the Mature Market,* Chicago: Probus Publishing Company, 1993, p. 23)

Many businesses offer senior discounts—if you ask—but they rarely advertise them. My research in the area of senior discounts has uncovered some interesting trends. There appears to be an under-utilization of senior citizen discounts for two main reasons. In a survey I conducted of age 50 and over Texas seniors in senior activity centers, 72 percent responded that they don't use discounts as much as they could either because they don't know who gives discounts and they don't know how to find out about them, or sales clerks don't offer them discounts. Thus, shoppers don't know where to find senior discounts and merchants fear offending customers, so they don't *offer* senior discounts. In the survey, these same seniors overwhelmingly agreed that if they knew where to find discounts and when they were offered, they would use them. Seventy-three percent responded they would even change the places they do business to receive senior citizen discounts!

This directory will identify which Texas businesses offer discounts, free goods and services, or good deals for people age 50 and better so you can confidently take advantage of them. You won't find this information anywhere else. I looked all over Texas.

Whether you see yourself as a senior or not, you are a discriminating shopper who wants the best value for your time and money. Time is the new currency of the '90s. Businesses offer discounts to remain competitive and to attract and keep your business. Astute business owners listed in this book have recognized the enormous buying potential of Texas seniors and have responded with senior discounts.

This guide will let you in on some of Texas' best kept secrets. Texas seniors and seniors all over the country are enjoying discounts at restaurants, grocery stores, ice cream parlors, golf courses, attorneys, banks, and even on their taxes! Why shouldn't you?

How to Use
This Book

The book is organized by categories of businesses offering discounts or good deals in Texas. Each business listing provides details about the discounts offered to seniors, including:

- products or services offered
- times when the discount is offered
- age requirement (they range from age 45 to 66)
- cities in which the discount is available (Index by Cities)
- any restrictions that may apply
- toll-free numbers and Internet addresses

Stop for a moment and flip to the Index by Cities at the end this book. The Index lists 495 Texas towns and cities, the businesses offering the discounts in each town, and the page on which the discounts are described. As you read this book, refer to the Index to find out whether a particular business is located in your city.

Addresses and phone numbers for businesses with only one or two locations are listed in the main part of the book. If a business is a national chain or has locations in several cities throughout Texas, the Index will tell you in which cities it is located. You can find the exact address and phone number in your telephone book or by calling the toll-free number provided. Because of the sheer numbers, entries for fast food restaurants discussed in the chapter, Restaurants and Fast Food, were not included in the Index.

The American free enterprise system is one of small businesses, corporations, and franchises. While one location of a franchise may offer a discount, another one may not. Discounts are often at the owner's or manager's discretion. Be aware that these offers may change or be eliminated at any time without notice, so it's a good idea to verify the discount before you want to use it.

In doing the research for this book, I found that many businesses I contacted didn't have a senior discount, until I called. There are probably a few discounts out there I missed, so be sure to ask. If nothing else, asking may encourage the business to reconsider its policy. While I have frequented many of the businesses listed, you will have to be the final judge of their quality and usefulness. It's my intention to update this book periodically, so if you find a discount that should be included, or one that has changed, please contact me at:

Web page: http://www.angelfire.com/biz/seniordiscount
e-mail: txauthor@yahoo.com
Mailing address: Gulf Publishing Company
       Book Division
       P.O. Box 2608
       Houston, TX 77252-2608

Also, remember in this electronic information age everything written and published is out-of-date almost the moment you receive it. Your telephone directory and your daily newspaper are obsolete before you even open them. Prior to publication, all of the discounts, locations, and phone numbers were verified; however, the market forces that drive a business to offer discounts can cause it to change or eliminate them as well. These discounts and offers are at participating locations only and are at the discretion of the business owners.

Airlines and Car Rental

AIRLINES

GENERAL GUIDELINES

Most airlines offer senior travelers some type of discount. The two main services are coupon books or discounts on individual fares. Often there are deeper discounts for advance purchase or other seasonal inducements, so be sure to ask for the best fare.

Most of the airlines offering a percentage-off-the-ticket discount will allow one or more traveling companions to enjoy the same discount regardless of their ages. Also, most of the discount coupon books are good for one year, but when they are about to expire, many airlines will issue you a ticket that is good for an additional year. The coupon book price typically includes tax, but when you exchange coupons for tickets, you'll need to pay the airport use tax which is generally less than $12.

There will be different restrictions among the airlines regarding blackout dates (dates when you cannot use the coupons), length of time coupons are valid, locations where coupons are valid, and whether traveling companions can enjoy the same senior discount. Call the toll-free 800 numbers for details. Most of the airlines have a brochure they're happy to mail to you about their program.

AMERICA WEST*

Based in Phoenix, Arizona, America West offers their senior passengers a Senior Saver Pack coupon book for $450 which includes four coupons. They also offer a discount on selected fares.

AGE:	62 and 65
DISCOUNT:	10% off applicable fare or coupon book
PHONE:	800-235-9292 (after 10 a.m. CST)
INTERNET:	http://www.americawest.com

America West has service in the following Texas locations:

- Austin
- Brownsville
- Corpus Christi
- Dallas/Fort Worth
- El Paso
- Harlingen
- Houston
- McAllen
- San Antonio

AMERICAN AIRLINES

This Dallas-based carrier offers their four-coupon Senior Traveler Coupon Book for $596, and they also offer seniors a 10% discount on most flights.

AGE:	62
DISCOUNT:	10% off applicable fare or coupon book
PHONE:	800-237-7981
INTERNET:	http://www.americanair.com

Senior Traveler Coupons are good for travel anywhere in the continental United States, San Juan, St. Thomas, and St. Croix. Except for travel to Hawaii, one coupon is required each direction. For travel to Hawaii, you'll use two coupons each way, or your entire coupon book.

---

* (Source: *Senior Saver Pack,* America West Airlines)

Seniors may stand by with these coupons at any time, but for confirmed reservations, you must call 14 days in advance. If you don't show up for your confirmed reservations, there is a $50 penalty.

American Airlines also offers seniors a 10% discount on most flights. Only the person paying for the tickets and making the reservations must be 62 or older to get the discount for his or her party.

CONQUEST AIRLINES

Austin-based Conquest Airlines offers a 10% discount off the lowest applicable fare for senior travelers.

AGE: 62
DISCOUNT: 10% off lowest applicable fare
PHONE: 800-772-0860
INTERNET: http://www.conquest.com

Conquest Airlines serves the following eight Texas cities:

- Abilene
- Austin
- Beaumont
- Corpus Christi
- Laredo
- San Antonio
- San Angelo
- Tyler

CONTINENTAL*

Continental is headquartered in Houston and offers a 10% discount to senior travelers. They offer a Freedom Passport Coupon Program. The Freedom Passport Program is quite extensive and can include European and Central American travel at an additional cost.

* (Source: *Freedom Passport and Freedom Trips*, Continental)

AGE: 62
DISCOUNT: 10% off applicable fare or coupon book
PHONE: 800-248-8996
INTERNET: http://www.flycontinental.com

Continental offers a book of four one-way coupons for $579 and a book of eight one-way coupons for $1,079. You'll exchange one Freedom Passport coupon for each one-way ticket for travel within the mainland U.S., Canada, Mexico, and the Caribbean (including San Juan and Puerto Rico). Travel to and from Alaska or Hawaii requires two certificates per one-way-trip.

In addition, Continental offers a 10% discount on most flights to senior travelers and one additional traveling companion.

DELTA AIR LINES*

Atlanta-based Delta Air Lines has the best-written and most detailed information about their "Young at Heart" program of the airlines surveyed. Much of that information is reproduced here. Delta offers a 10% discount to seniors at least 62 years of age and one traveling companion, and they offer Senior Travel Coupon Books.

AGE: 62
DISCOUNT: 10% off applicable fare or coupon book
PHONE: 800-221-1212
INTERNET: http://www.delta-air.com

Discount Fares

Details of discount fares are as follows:

- Make reservations as usual, abiding by the rules of the fare you choose (this discount applies to most fares).
- Save 10% on your traveling partner's fare, regardless of traveling partner's age, except as noted.

---

* (Source: *You're Only Young Twice*, Delta Air Lines)

- Travel between cities within the U.S. or between cities in the U.S. and any of these Delta destinations, except as noted:

Amsterdam	Athens
Barcelona	Berlin*
Bermuda	Brussels
Bucharest	Budapest
Canada	Copenhagen**
Dublin	Frankfurt*
Geneva*	Istanbul
London	Madrid
Manchester	Mexico
Milan	Moscow
Munich*	Nagoya*
Nice*	Paris*
Prague	Rome
St. Croix	St. Petersburg
St. Thomas	San Juan
Seoul*	Shannon
Stuttgart*	The Bahamas
Tokyo	Vienna*
Warsaw	Zurich

Delta Senior Travel Coupon Books contain four one-way coupons at a cost of $596. The coupons are good for one year from the date of purchase, and coupons may be exchanged for tickets at any time.

Delta Senior Travel Coupon Books may be used for domestic destinations of the Delta Connection carriers as well. You'll exchange one coupon for each one-way ticket for travel within the 48 contiguous states. Travel to Hawaii or Alaska requires the entire book of four coupons.

---

* Discount fare applies for all flights originating in the U.S. only
** Does not apply for companion travel

SOUTHWEST AIRLINES*

Dallas-based Southwest Airlines has had a senior program for over 20 years. Their Senior Fares are particular to the flight and are not based on a set discount percentage.

AGE: 65
DISCOUNT: Senior Fares by flight destination
PHONE: 800-435-9792
INTERNET: http://www.iflyswa.com

Southwest's Senior Fares are offered on every flight, every day of the week; however, seats are limited. Valid identification proving you are 65 or older may be required at the time of travel, and reservations are required. Reserved flights may be changed if senior seats are available on the alternate flight(s) you want.

Advance purchase of tickets isn't necessary, but fares are subject to change until the tickets are purchased. Southwest Airlines' Senior Fare tickets may be purchased one-way or round-trip and are fully refundable. Be prepared for Southwest Airlines' new "ticketless" traveling. You just pay your fare with a major credit card, receive your confirmation number, and you're ready to fly. When doing this by phone, I strongly recommend you request and receive a written confirmation in the mail. Southwest Airlines also has a handy "Travel Tips for Seniors" they'll be happy to mail or fax to you.

UNITED AIRLINES**

United Airlines offers seniors who are 62 or older the Silver TravelPac coupon book and a 10% discount off any fare anywhere they fly.

AGE: 62
DISCOUNT: 10% off applicable fares
PHONE: 800-241-6522
INTERNET: http://www.ual.com

---

 * (Source: *We Were Senior When Senior Wasn't Cool*, Southwest Airlines)
** (Source: *Silver TravelPac - Big Savings for Travelers Age 62 Plus*, United Airlines)

The Silver TravelPac coupon book contains four one-way coupons for $596. Coupons must be redeemed for a ticket within one year, but those tickets are also good for another year. Reservations must be made 14 days in advance of travel. Travel to most destinations requires one coupon each way. Travel to Hawaii requires two coupons each way.

United Airlines also offers seniors its Silver Wings Plus discount program (see Senior Organizations).

U.S. Air

With U.S. Air's Golden Opportunities program, seniors 65 and better can purchase a travel coupon book with four one-way coupons for $596. They will also receive a 10% discount off most fares, and that discount will be extended to a traveling companion.

AGE: 65
DISCOUNT: 10% off applicable fares or coupon book
PHONE: 800-428-4322
INTERNET: http://www.usair.com

CAR RENTAL

GENERAL GUIDELINES*

Never rent a car without getting a special promotional rate or discount. Car rental agencies give discounts to many senior travel clubs such as AARP, Sears's Mature Outlook, and Montgomery Ward's Y.E.S. Club. If you belong to any travel club, be sure to ask if they offer a discount for your organization. Refer to Senior Organizations for information about these over-50 memberships.

Most agencies give Frequent Flyer mileage to members and some give discounts. When you call to rent a car, be sure to have

* (Source: Heilman, J. R. *Unbelievably Good Deals & Great Adventures that You Absolutely Can't Get Unless You're Over 50.* Chicago: Contemporary Books, Inc., 1988, pp. 187–89)

all your travel club ID numbers ready. They'll key in your ID number to see if a discount is available for the date, location, and type of car you are seeking. Discounts may not be available due to the location, time of year, and availability of cars.

AVIS RENT-A-CAR

AGE:	50
DISCOUNT:	5–15%
PHONE:	800-331-1212
INTERNET:	http://www.avis.com
HONORS:	Avis Half-Century Discount
	AARP
	Frequent Flyer
	Mature Outlook

BUDGET CAR AND TRUCK RENTAL

AGE:	50
DISCOUNT:	10%
PHONE:	800-527-0700
INTERNET:	http://www.budgetrentacar.com
HONORS:	AARP
	Mature Outlook
	Y.E.S.

DOLLAR RENT A CAR

AGE:	65 (50 for AARP)
DISCOUNT:	Varies according to location
PHONE:	800-800-4000
INTERNET:	http://www.dollarcar.com
HONORS:	Dollar Rent-A-Car Senior Discount
	AARP

HERTZ RENT A CAR

AGE:	50
DISCOUNT:	5–15%
PHONE:	800-654-3131
INTERNET:	http://www.hertz.com
HONORS:	AARP
	Mature Outlook
	Y.E.S.

NATIONAL CAR RENTAL

AGE:	50
DISCOUNT:	10%
PHONE:	800-227-7368
INTERNET:	http://www.nationalcar.com
HONORS:	AARP
	Frequent Flyer
	Mature Outlook
	Y.E.S.

U-HAUL CO.

In addition to renting trucks and trailers, U-Haul is the second largest operator of self-storage facilities in the country. They have a program called Storage at Destination offered on an *as-available* basis to renters of one-way vehicles. When you make arrangements for this program at your place of origin, and when space is available at your U-Haul destination, U-Haul will provide renters with 30 days of free storage.

PHONE:	800-528-0463

Auto, Home, and Garden

Auto Express*

As members of the Y.E.S. (Years of Extra Savings) program offered by Montgomery Ward, seniors 55 and up can save on auto repairs at Auto Express stores that are located in many Montgomery Ward Stores. Membership in Y.E.S. costs $34.95 a year, or $2.99 a month. (See Shopping for more details)

AGE: 55
DISCOUNT: 10%
PHONE: 800-421-5396

Services available for most vehicles include:

- Oil change
- Shocks/struts installation
- A/C recharge
- Brake service
- Wheel alignment
- Fuel injection cleaning

* (Source: *Y.E.S. If You're 55 or Over!*, Montgomery Ward)

- Electrical systems
- Tune-up
- Computerized engine analysis

The 10% discount may not be used in conjunction with any other discount or coupon. It's not valid for sales tax, delivery, service contracts, or the Montgomery Ward Clearance Outlet Center. Your local Montgomery Ward store can give you a brochure and take your application.

BRAKE SPECIALISTS, INC.

Brake Specialists, Inc. provides total under-car care. They provide services for alignments, brakes, shocks, struts, air conditioning at some locations, and oil changes at some locations. Discounts are offered at all Austin locations and at the Round Rock location.

AGE: 55
DISCOUNT: 10%

JIFFY LUBE

Jiffy Lube performs routine car care maintenance checks, such as oil change, transmission, lubrication, and fluid checks. Most locations also provide state inspections.

AGE: 45
DISCOUNT: 10%
INTERNET: http://www.jiffylube.com

QUICK LUBE

For years, Wednesday has been Senior Citizens' Discount Day at Quick Lube. This discount is for their standard full-service, 15-point lubrication, oil and oil filter change.

AGE: 60
DISCOUNT: $3 off Wednesdays only

In business for 18 years, Quick Lube is a full-service automotive preventive maintenance provider. They also offer service on:

- Air systems
- Differential
- Transfer cases
- Fuel system
- Air conditioning

- Transmissions
- Change lubricant
- Radiator
- State inspections

Discounts are offered at all Austin locations, Lockhart, and San Antonio. Be sure to ask.

NATIONAL TRANSMISSION CENTERS*

With over 40 years of experience, National Transmission Centers offer automatic and standard transmission and clutch repairs for foreign and domestic automobiles, trucks, RVs, and 4x4s.

AGE:	63
DISCOUNT:	10% off parts and labor
ADDRESS:	27202 Tomball Pkwy.
	Tomball
	281-351-4633
	1745 Kuykendahl
	Spring
	281-376-4633

National Transmission Centers will sometimes hold checks until payday for seniors for emergency work, and they also offer the following free services:

- Towing with internal automatic transmission repairs
- Road test
- External analysis
- Local shuttle rides to home or work

* (Source: Internet Web Page http://www.houstoncentral.com/national.htm)

Home and Garden

Ability Plumbing Co.

If you're 60 or better in the Houston area and you need a plumber, call Bill Ford, owner and master plumber.

AGE: 60
DISCOUNT: $10 off total bill
PHONE: 713-688-3513

Ability Plumbing Co. offers complete repair and service. They will repair or replace water and gas lines and have water heaters and shower pans. They've been a family-owned and operated business since 1973.

All Electric

Seniors in Cedar Creek and the Bastrop County area can get a discount on electrical and air conditioning service with All Electric. This licensed and bonded company has 24-hour service.

AGE: 65
DISCOUNT: 10% off parts and labor
PHONE: 512-914-0006
                512-469-1374 (digital pager)

Angelina Roofing Co., Inc.

Angelina Roofing Co. in Lufkin offers commercial, industrial, and residential roofing services with a senior citizen discount. They have over 25 years of experience and can do your roofing, remodeling, or siding job. They're licensed and bonded and accept VISA and MasterCard. Call owner Jim McCarter for a free estimate.

ADDRESS: 2310 Teer
                Lufkin
PHONE: 409-632-1993

BAY AREA CHIMNEY SWEEP

In Houston, if you need one of the following services, call Bay Area Chimney Sweep. They offer senior discounts.

- Chimney cleaning
- Chimney repairs
- Firebox repairs
- Caps installed
- Relining of flue
- Gas logs installed

PHONE: 281-471-1409

BUILDERS SQUARE

You'll find everything you need for the garden or any home-improvement project at Builders Square. For a senior discount on everything except lumber and already reduced items, visit them on Tuesdays.

AGE: 55
DISCOUNT: 10% Tuesday only

EAGLE AIR CONDITIONING SERVICE

In Houston, owner David L. Moore will provide you with heating and air conditioning installation, sales, and repair with a senior discount.

AGE: 65
DISCOUNT: 10%
PHONE: 713-996-1271

FOX SERVICE COMPANY, INC.

This Austin-area company gives seniors a discount on parts and labor for repairs on air conditioning, heating, plumbing, electricity, and pool/spa services. They also provide lawn care.

AGE: 65
DISCOUNT: 10%

ADDRESS: 4300 S. Congress Ave.
               Austin
PHONE: 512-442-6782

FURROWS/PAYLESS CASHWAYS

To make your building job easier, visit your local Furrows or Payless Cashways. They offer a 10% senior discount on Tuesdays on everything except power tools, special orders, and lumber at participating stores.

AGE: 55
DISCOUNT: 10% Tuesday only

GENERAL IONICS OF AUSTIN

General Ionics can provide you with a whole-house water treatment system at a discount. They have plans to expand the number of their stores in the I-35 corridor from Austin to Dallas and San Antonio.

AGE: 50
DISCOUNT: 10% off sales and installation
ADDRESS: 12176 N. Mopac Suite E
               Austin
PHONE: 512-833-7498 (in Austin)
               800-397-1511 (outside Austin calling area)

J&R ENTERPRISES*

For seniors living in Brownsville and the Rio Grande Valley, J&R Enterprises provides tree trimming, shaping, and removal and lawn maintenance for commercial or residential properties. Weekly, monthly, or annual contracts are available. They accept VISA, MasterCard, or Discover.

* (Source: Internet: http://www.xanadu2.net/trees/billing.html)

```
AGE:         65
DISCOUNT:    10%
PHONE:       210-748-4155
INTERNET:    http://www.xanadu2.net/trees/index.html
```

620 STORAGE

If you need long-term storage in the Austin area, give 620 Storage a call.

```
AGE:         55
DISCOUNT:    $10 per month discount
ADDRESS:     12120-B Hwy. 620 North
             Austin
PHONE:       512-918-1619
```

SOPHORA LAWN SERVICE

For commercial and residential landscape maintenance or design and installation in the Austin area, give Chuck Webb and company a call.

```
AGE:         55
DISCOUNT:    10%
PHONE:       512-301-1557
```

THE HANDY MANN

Barry Mann, The Handy Mann, will give seniors a discount on home remodeling. They provide plumbing, painting, carpentry, ramps for wheelchair access, grab bars, fences, and decks. They'll consider other jobs as well.

```
AGE:         60
DISCOUNT:    25%
ADDRESS:     10602 Denell Circle
             Austin
PHONE:       512-837-5007
             512-450-5555 (digital pager)
```

THE HOME DEPOT

This is a great store to find everything for the home from lumber and plants to chandeliers. They also have employees who are extremely knowledgeable about home remodeling and repair projects. The Home Depot's policy is to match the lowest price offered locally, including advertised prices and prices you can get anywhere else with a senior discount.

VERSA TILE

Owned and operated by two brothers in the Austin area since 1991, Versa Tile will do anything you want with any type of tile or marble in the Austin metropolitan area. If you want tile in your kitchen, shower, wherever—their team can handle it. They've been gaining acceptance with *anti-slip* tile and bathtub treatments and offer special discounts on those products.

AGE:	55
DISCOUNT:	10% off labor (and pass along any manufacturer's senior discounts on tiles/marble)
PHONE:	512-502-8944

WOLFE/GARDENLAND/SUNBELT NURSERY

Make this store your landscaping headquarters with a huge supply of trees, native and xeriscape plants, and supplies.

AGE:	62
DISCOUNT:	15% off regular-priced merchandise Wednesdays only

This discount is not available for sale merchandise, clearance items, etc. To take advantage of this discount, just present your driver's license (or other form of identification that includes a birth date) at the store. The store associate will give you a decal that sticks onto your driver's license, a credit card, or onto a Wolfe Nursery/Sunbelt Nursery business card. The discount can be given at that time. There's no waiting period.

Banks and Insurance Companies

BANKS

BANK ONE*

Bank One provides the Classic One checking account for seniors 55 and better. This account has the following features:

- Earns interest
- No $10 monthly service fee if combined balance of $5,000 or more
- Unlimited transactions per month
- 24-hour access
- Free The One Card
- Monthly statement
- Optional overdraft protection
- Free Classic One wallet checks
- No fee American Express Travelers Cheques and Cheques for Two
- No fee money orders

---

* (Source: *Could One of Our Checking Choices Sharpen Up Your Finances?* Bank One)

FROST BANK*

Frost Bank offers Advantage 50 and Advantage 50 Plus checking accounts. Both require $500 minimum to open an account, and both are interest-earning checking accounts.

PHONE: 800-233-9874
INTERNET: frostbank@frostbank.com (e-mail)
                    http://www.frostbank.com (Web page)

Advantage 50 has the following features:

- Earns competitive interest
- Unlimited check-writing privileges
- Free ReadyBank ATM card
- Free first order of 200 checks
- No annual fee VISA or MasterCard
- Free cashier's checks, money orders, and travelers checks
- $10 discount on safe deposit box
- $100,000 Common Carrier Accidental Death Insurance
- Annual local merchants coupon book
- Semi-annual travel magazine with articles and discounts
- Nationwide discounts on lodging, entertainment, and car rentals
- Overdraft protection through another checking, savings, Creditline, or money market account
- Credit card and Key Ring Protection
- Total statement that provides clear, reduced copies of each check written on the account

If your minimum daily balance for the month is $1,000 or more, there is no service charge. Or, if the combined minimum daily balances in your checking, savings, Money Market Account,

---

* (Source: *Checking Choices*, Frost Bank)

or CD are $10,000 or more, there is no service charge. Below these minimum daily balances, the monthly service charge is $8.

Advantage 50 Plus offers all of the Advantage 50 benefits, plus:

- Free personalized checks
- $10,000 Accidental Death Insurance
- Discount pharmacy and eye wear
- Traveler's Advantage Discounts

The monthly membership fee is $4. If your minimum daily balance for the month is $1,000 or more, there is no service charge. Or, if the combined minimum daily balances in your checking, savings, Money Market Account, or CD are $10,000 or more, there is no service charge. Below these minimum daily balances, the monthly service charge is $8.

Frost Bank locations may be found in Austin, Corpus Christi, Galveston, Houston, San Antonio, and Sugar Land.

NATIONSBANK*

Reward 55 is a NationsBank checking account for seniors 55 and over. The minimum initial deposit to open the account is $100, and the minimum book balance to obtain the disclosed annual percentage yield is $1,000. With Reward 55 you'll receive:

- Free custom, wallet-style personal checks (200 per order)
- Unlimited check writing
- Only one depositor must be 50 or over to meet the age requirement for a joint account
- Competitive rate of interest when your book balance is $1,000 or more
- Interest is compounded monthly on collected balances

---

* (Source: *Personal Accounts and Services*, NationsBank)

You can avoid a monthly maintenance fee of $6 by meeting one of the following balance requirements:

Minimum daily balance in Reward 55:	$ 1,500
Minimum daily balance in Regular Savings:	$ 2,500
Minimum daily balance in a Money Market Savings Account:	$ 3,500
Minimum balance in a NationsBank CD:	$10,000

TEXAS COMMERCE BANK*

Texas Commerce Bank offers the OnePlus50 account as a way to reward people 50 and better for banking at TCB. It offers special features designed for people who are at least 50 years of age.

AGE: 50
PHONE: 800-235-8522

With OnePlus50, customers:

- Receive rewards and special recognition for the amount of business they do
- Receive free personal checks
- Receive savings on travel, health care, and entertainment
- Pay less in fees
- Earn interest on checking
- Receive lower rates on loans and credit cards
- Receive bonus rates on CDs
- Receive personal attention when they need it
- Receive an ATM card

* (Source: *ONEPLUS50 Your Way,* Texas Commerce Bank)

UNION STATE BANK*

This bank has been serving central Texans for 68 years. Union State Bank Silver Advantage Checking Accounts require no minimum balance with no charges for monthly maintenance fees, Silver Advantage checks, money orders, or cashier's checks. There's also no charge for a small safe deposit box or you may receive credit toward a larger one.

Silver Advantage NOW accounts (interest-bearing checking) have tiers to give customers the maximum flexibility, ready access to funds and unlimited check writing with a minimum balance of $1,500. These accounts include all the Silver Advantage checking account privileges plus interest. NOW customers may also participate in the Silver Advantage Travel & Social Club and its once-a-month special activity.

Union State Bank locations are in Florence, Georgetown, and Killeen.

INSURANCE COMPANIES

GENERAL GUIDELINES

Insurance regulations differ from state to state, but drivers in Texas often see a decline in their insurance rates as they mature. Many insurance companies reduce rates on some portions of your auto insurance and home owners insurance as you age. Some, however, *increase* your auto insurance after age 70. Included here is information about the larger insurance companies. Call your insurance agent for details on your policy.

AETNA

Home:	No reduction based on aging	
Auto:	Age 50–64	Approximately 5% reduction
	Age 70+	Approximately 10% increase

* (Source: *Senior News,* May 1996)

ALLSTATE

Home:	Age 55	Approximately 5% reduction
Auto:	Age 55	Unspecified reduction

NATIONWIDE

Home:	No reduction based on aging	
Auto:	Age 55	Approximately 10% reduction

STATE FARM

Home:	No reduction based on aging	
Auto:	Age 50	Approximately 10–15% reduction

USAA

Home:	No reduction based on aging	
Auto:	Age 50	Approximately 16% reduction
	Age 60	Reduction declines
	Age 75	Reduction declines

Camping and Wildlife Pursuits

FISHING AND HUNTING

FISHING LICENSES*

A resident fishing license is required of any Texas resident who fishes in the public waters of Texas, unless:

- They hold another fishing license considered valid by the Texas Parks and Wildlife Department (TPWD), or
- They meet certain restrictions outlined in the *Texas Parks & Wildlife Outdoor Annual*

All members of the U.S. Armed Forces on active duty and their dependents are considered residents.

Resident fishing licenses are issued by the TPWD, and there are many exceptions and restrictions. Under most circumstances, you'll also need to purchase either a salt water stamp or a fresh water stamp.

The good news is Texas residents who reached 65 years of age before September 1, 1995, do not need this license or the stamps (unless you want to fish for red drum. Call the toll-free number for details). Texas residents who turn 65 on or after September 1, 1995, aren't eligible for free fishing licenses, but they are eligible for a deep discount.

* (Source: *Texas Parks & Wildlife Outdoor Annual 1996-1997*. Austin: The Publishing Partnership, a division of Texas Monthly, USA, 1996)

AGE: 65
COST: $6 ($19 for under 65 and non-Texas residents)
PHONE: 800-792-1112
INTERNET: http://www.tpwd.state.tx.us

Call the toll-free number and ask the TPWD to mail you a free copy of the *Texas Parks & Wildlife Outdoor Annual.* This booklet includes all the details on hunting and fishing licenses, official hunting and fishing regulations, hunting and fishing yarns, and county listings of hunting seasons and limits.

HUNTING LICENSES*

A resident hunting license is required of any Texas resident who hunts in Texas, unless:

- They hold another hunting license considered valid by the Texas Parks and Wildlife Department (TPWD), or
- They meet certain restrictions outlined in the *Texas Parks & Wildlife Outdoor Annual*

All members of the U.S. Armed Forces on active duty and their dependents are considered residents.

Hunting licenses are issued by the TPWD, and there are many exceptions and restrictions. Under most circumstances, you'll also need to purchase one of the following stamps:

- Archery Stamp
- Muzzleloader Hunting Stamp
- Texas Waterfowl Stamp
- Turkey Stamp
- White-winged Dove Stamp
- Federal Migratory Bird Hunting and Conservation Stamp
- Federal Sandhill Crane Hunting Permit—Free

---

* (Source: *Texas Parks & Wildlife Outdoor Annual 1996–1997,* Austin: The Publishing Partnership, a division of Texas Monthly, USA, 1996)

Texas residents who reached 65 years of age before September 1, 1995, do not need this license or the stamps. Texas residents who turn 65 on or after September 1, 1995, aren't eligible for free fishing licenses, but they are eligible for a deep discount.

```
AGE:         65
COST:        $6 ($19 for under 65 and non-Texas residents)
PHONE:       800-792-1112
INTERNET:    http://www.tpwd.state.tx.us
```

Call the toll-free number and ask the TPWD to mail you a free copy of the *Texas Parks & Wildlife Outdoor Annual*. This booklet includes all the details on hunting and fishing licenses, official hunting and fishing regulations, hunting and fishing tales, and county listings of hunting seasons and limits.

RECREATION AREAS

GOLDEN AGE PASSPORT*

The Golden Age Passport is a lifetime entrance pass for seniors to national parks and forests, monuments, historic sites, recreation areas, and national wildlife refuges that normally charge an entrance fee.

```
AGE:         62
COST:        $10 one-time fee
```

You can acquire this passport at any federal park area where an entrance fee is charged. It's available only to citizens or permanent residents of the United States. It not only admits the senior, but also any accompanying passengers in his or her private vehicle. In most cases, if you're entering on foot, the passport admits the pass

* (Source: *Federal Recreation Passport Program*, National Park Service and *National Parks in Texas*, Southwest Region Department of the Interior)

holder, spouse, and children. Your Golden Age Passport will also provide a 50% discount on federal-use fees charged for facilities and services such as camping, swimming, parking, and boat launching.

For further information contact:

Southwest Region
National Park Service
P. O. Box 728
Santa Fe, NM 87504-0728
505-988-6012

NATIONAL FORESTS IN TEXAS*

These forests are administered by the U. S. Forest Service and primitive camping is allowed, except where posted. No electric, water, or sewer hookups are provided, and hunting and fishing is regulated by the Texas Parks & Wildlife Department. Self-deposit of fees is provided for fee areas for overnight camping or day use of developed swimming beaches.

For more detailed information about the individual recreation areas in all Texas parks and forests, contact the State Department of Highways and Public Transportation. Upon request, they will mail you free copies of the following publications:

- State Travel Guide
- State Map
- Accommodation Guide
- Campground Guide
- Calendar of Events for the coming quarter (printed for winter, summer, spring, and fall)

PHONE: 800-452-9292
INTERNET: http://traveltex.com (e-mail)
                   http://www.dot.state.tx.us (Web Page)

---

* (Source: *Texas Travel Handbook,* State Department of Highways and Public Transportation, Travel & Information Division, 1996)

Physical Address
State Department of Highways and Public Transportation
Travel & Information Division
1101 E. Anderson Ln.
Austin, TX 78752

Mailing Address
P. O. Box 764
Austin, TX 78763-5064

Angelina National Forest. This is the smallest national forest in Texas with 154,916 acres in Angelina, Jasper, Nacogdoches, and San Augustine counties. The rural town of Zavalla, which grew around Concord Church before the Civil War, is located within the boundary of the Angelina National Forest. It has the following recreation areas: Bouton Lake, Boykin Springs, Caney Creek, Harvey Creek, Sandy Creek, and Sawmill Hiking Trail.

Davy Crockett National Forest. This national forest is composed of 161,497 acres in Houston and Trinity counties with the following recreation areas: Big Slough Canoe Train, 4-C's Hiking Trail, Kickapoo, Neches Bluff, and Ratcliff Lake.

Sabine National Forest. This is the largest national forest in Texas with 188,220 acres in Jasper, Sabine, San Augustine, Newton, and Shelby counties. It has the following recreation areas: East Hamilton, Indian Mounds, Lakeview, Ragtown, Red Hills Lake, Snyders, and Willow Oak.

Sam Houston National Forest. This forest covers 160,443 acres in Montgomery, San Jacinto, and Walker counties and offers these recreation areas: Big Creek Scenic Area, Cagle, Double Lake, Kelly Pound, Lone Star Hiking Trail, Scott's Ridge, and Stubblefield Lake.

NATIONAL PARKS IN TEXAS*

The Alibates Flint Quarries National Monument. Many thousands of years ago Native Americans discovered the Alibates flint deposits exposed on the hillside over what is now Lake Meredith. This lonely hillside became the center of a prehistoric quarrying "industry." This superb, beautifully colored flint was used to make stone knives, projectile points, and other tools archaeologists find throughout the Southwest.

> Alibates Flint Quarries National Monument
> c/o Lake Meredith National Recreation Area
> P. O. Box 1438
> Fritch, TX 79036
> 806-857-3151

Amistad National Recreation Area. Amistad, meaning "friendship," is the place where the United States and Mexico cooperated to build Amistad Dam on the Rio Grande in 1969. A lake with an 850-mile shoreline was created that today provides a sunny playground of boating and fishing for recreation enthusiasts from Mexico and the United States.

> Amistad National Recreation Area
> P. O. Box 420367
> Del Rio, TX 78842-0367
> 512-775-7491

Big Bend National Park. One of the great national parks, Big Bend is the place where the Rio Grande makes the "big bend" into Mexico and turns north again. Here is the Chihuahuan Desert, vast, remote, stark, and beautiful. Desert mountains contrast with the flats below, punctuated by abrupt canyons of

---

* (Source: National Parks in Texas, Southwest Region, Department of the Interior)

the Rio Grande. In addition to the stunning scenery, the park celebrates the unique culture of a remote borderland.

Big Bend National Park
Big Bend National Park, TX 79834
915-477-2251

Big Thicket National Preserve. Early pioneers were in awe as they entered the dense forest they called "The Big Thicket," where the swamps of east Texas meet the plains. Those who settled there, creating the region's unique culture, found the "thicket" demanding, but also rewarding with an amazing diversity of plants and animals. This is nature at its richest, whether it be birds and butterflies flickering through forest dimness, riots of wildflowers, or a raccoon investigating the water's edge. The preserve has been designated a "Man and the Biosphere" reserve by the United Nations Educational, Scientific, and Cultural Organization (UNESCO). This designation is reserved for areas of unique significance for their biological diversity and has been given to only 400 areas in the world. Big Bend National Park and Big Thicket National Preserve are the only two "Man and the Biosphere" reserves in Texas.

Big Thicket National Preserve
3785 Milam
Beaumont, TX 77701
409-839-2691

Chamizal National Monument. The memorial commemorates the Chamizal Convention of 1963 that resolved a conflict of nearly a century between Mexico and the United States regarding a land ownership dispute that poisoned international relations. An historical museum and films retell the history of the international border. Multicultural programs are provided weekly in the small theatre, outdoor amphitheater, and the Lienzo de Charros (Charreada arena).

Chamizal National Memorial
800 South San Marcial
El Paso, TX 79905
915-532-7273 (Dial 101)

Fort Davis National Historic Site. It was a key post in the West Texas defense system, guarding immigrants and tradesmen on the San Antonio-El Paso Road. Fort Davis was manned by black troops for many of the years it was active. These troops, called "Buffalo Soldiers" because of their curly hair, fought with great distinction in the Indian Wars. Henry O. Flipper, the first black graduate of West Point, served at Fort Davis in the early 1880s.

Fort Davis National Historic Site
P. O. Box 1456
Fort Davis, TX 79734
915-426-3225

Guadalupe Mountains National Park. A mountain mass of Permian limestone rises abruptly from the surrounding desert and contains one of the most extensive fossil reefs on record. Deep canyons cut through this exposed fossil reef and provide a rare opportunity for geological study. Special points of interest are McKittrick Canyon, a fragile riparian environment, and Guadalupe Peak, the highest in Texas.

Guadalupe Mountains National Park
H.C. 60, Box 400
Salt Flat, TX 79847-9400
915-828-3251

Lake Meredith National Recreation Area. This 50,000-acre outdoor recreation area was established for its natural, cultural, scientific, and recreation significance to the Texas Panhandle region. Its 21,000-acre top quality reservoir provides a scenic outdoor recreation experience. The area also includes 1,200 species of plant life, 200 species of birds, 33 mammals, three endangered species, and just over 400 documented archaeological sites.

Lake Meredith National Recreation Area
P. O. Box 1438
Fritch, TX 79036
806-857-3151

Lyndon B. Johnson National Historical Park. Visit the Texas Hill Country where Lyndon Baines Johnson, 36th President of the United States, was born and grew up. Preserved here are his birthplace, boyhood home, the LBJ Ranch, and his pioneer ancestors' ranch headquarters. President Johnson returned here often during his 37 years of public service to rest and enjoy the place he called his home, the "Texas White House."

Lyndon B. Johnson National Historic Park
P. O. Box 329
Johnson City, TX 78636
512-868-7128

Padre Island National Seashore. Noted for its wide sand beaches, excellent fishing, abundant bird and marine life, this barrier island stretches along the Gulf Coast for 67.5 miles. Padre Island is a playground and a place to see nature at its most wonderful.

Padre Island National Seashore
9405 South Padre Island Drive
Corpus Christi, TX 78418-5597
512-949-8173

Rio Grande Wild and Scenic River. It's a 191.2-mile strip on the American shore of the Rio Grande in the Chihuahuan Desert that protects the river. It begins in Big Bend National Park and continues downstream to the Terrell-Val Verde county line.

Rio Grande Wild and Scenic River
c/o Big Bend National Park
Big Bend National Park, TX 79835
915-477-2251

San Antonio Missions National Historic Park. The colonial mission was one of the principal institutions of settlement on Spain's northern frontier. Four of these missions, Concepcion, San Jose, San Juan, and Espada, along with the Espada dam and aqueduct (two of the best preserved remains of the Spanish Colonial irrigation system in the United States), are physical reminders of a glorious chapter in Spanish Colonial history. All were crucial elements to Spanish settlement on the Texas frontier. When Franciscan attempts to establish a chain of missions in East Texas in the late 1600s failed, the Spanish Crown ordered the missions transferred to the lush valley of the San Antonio River in 1731 where they flourished until secularization in 1824.

San Antonio Missions National Historic Park
2202 Roosevelt Avenue
San Antonio, TX 78210
512-229-5701

STATE PARKLANDS PASSPORT*

Whether you want to bake on a sun-drenched beach, observe exotic birds, backpack through rugged terrain, or study 4,000-year-old Indian pictographs, Texas has a state park for you.

The Texas State Parklands Passport, also known as the Bluebonnet Passport, is a windshield decal that allows all persons who reached 65 years of age before September 1, 1995, and vet-

---

* (Source: *Texas Travel Handbook,* State Department of Highways and Public Transportation, Travel & Information Division, 1996)

erans with a 60 percent or greater disability rating to enter Texas State Parks for free. There may be additional fees for camping, tours, or special activities fees, so use the phone numbers provided to call ahead.

Texas residents who turned 65 on or after September 1, 1995, are eligible for discounted entry fees; however, each park sets its own fees. Weekly, monthly, senior citizen, and seasonal discounts on camping are offered by most parks. In addition, premium (preferred) campsites, shelters, and cabins are available at some parks. Nonresidents who became 65 after September 1, 1995, pay the regular price.

The Texas Parks and Wildlife Department (TPWD) has several other passports worth investigating if you don't fit the profile for the Texas State Parklands Passport. Call the toll-free number for details.

The TPWD also has brochures and information available on every Texas State Park. Call the toll-free number to have them mail you brochures or answer questions. In addition, TPWD publishes *Texas Parks and Wildlife* magazine that is invaluable to Texas travelers. They even have a senior discount on their magazine! Seniors who have a Texas State Parklands Passport receive 12 issues a year for $10 compared to the regular price of 12 issues a year for $12.95.

800-792-1112: Parks, boating, fishing, hunting and wildlife, permits, passports, reservations, and Special Events Calendar
800-937-9393: *Texas Parks and Wildlife* magazine
INTERNET: http://www.magazine@tpwd.state.tx.us.com

State Forests in Texas*

There are four state forests in Texas, and they're managed by the Texas Forest Service that is part of the Texas A&M University

---

* (Source: *Texas Travel Handbook*, State Department of Highways and Public Transportation, Travel & Information Division, 1996)

System. These forests are wildlife refuges, and while no hunting is allowed, fishing is permitted in designated areas.

The Texas Forest Service operates Indian Mound Nursery near Alto and annually provides some 30 million seedlings to private landowners to reforest their land.

Fairchild State Forest. This forest was named for State Senator I. D. Fairchild of Lufkin and was originally owned by the State Prison System. The largest tract of this six-tract, 2,896-acre forest is 13 miles west of Rusk along U.S. 84. There's a small day-use area for hiking, fishing, and picnicking.

Jones State Forest. Five miles south of Conroe you'll find this 1,725-acre state forest area that is nesting site to the rare, red cockaded woodpecker. The forest offers a self-guided nature trail, fishing, swimming, cooking grills, and restrooms.

Kirby State Forest. This land was donated by John Henry Kirby, lumberman, in 1929. This 600-acre forest is located 14 miles south of Woodville and offers a lovely picnic area.

Siecke State Forest. The main tract of this two-tract forest is located five miles southeast of Kirbyville via U.S. 96 and F.M. 82. Fishing is allowed in Trout Creek as well as swimming and picnicking.

STATE PARKS IN TEXAS*

Albany

Fort Griffin State Historical Park
915-762-3592

Alto

Caddoan Mounds State
  Historical Park
409-858-3218

Anderson

Fanthorp Inn State Historical Park
Charge for tours only
409-873-2633

Atlanta

Atlanta State Park
903-796-6476

* (Source: *Texas State Parks Facility and Fee Guide*, Texas Parks and Wildlife)

Austin

Bright Leaf State Park
McKinney Falls Pkwy.
512-243-1643

McKinney Falls State Park
Swimming update: 512-243-0848
512-243-1643

Balmorhea

Balmorhea State Park
San Solomon Springs Courts
915-375-2370

Bandera

Hill Country State Natural Area
210-796-4413

Bastrop

Bastrop State Park
512-321-2101

Lake Bastrop State Park
512-321-2101

Baytown

Christmas Bay State Park
Undeveloped Gulf Beach
281-471-3200

Bend

Colorado Bend State Park
Cave tours
915-628-3240

Big Spring

Big Spring State Park
#1 Scenic Drive
915-263-4931

Blanco

Blanco State Park
210-833-4333

Boerne

Guadalupe River State Park &
    Honey Creek State
    Natural Area
Honey Creek State Natural Area
    Guided Tours
210-438-2656

Bonham

Bonham State Park
903-583-5022

Bracketville

Kickapoo Cavern State Park
210-563-2342

Brownwood

Lake Brownwood State Park
915-784-5223

Buffalo Gap

Abilene State Park
915-572-3204

Burnet

Inks Lake State Park
512-793-2223

Longhorn Cavern State Park
Daily Cavern Tours Schedule:
    512-756-6976
Charge for tours only
512-756-4680

Caddo

Possum Kingdom State Park
817-549-1803

Calliham

Choke Canyon State Park
Calliham Unit
512-786-3868

Canyon

Palo Duro Canyon State Park
Summer Drama "Texas"
806-488-2227

Castroville

Landmark Inn State Historical
    Park
210-931-2133

Cedar Hill

Cedar Hill State Park
972-291-3900

Centerville

Fort Boggy State Park
817-562-5533

Cleburne

Cleburne State Park
817-645-4215

Colorado City

Lake Colorado City State Park
915-728-3931

Concan

Garner State Park
210-232-6132

Conroe

Davis Hill State Park
281-471-3200

Cooper

Cooper Lake State Park
Doctors Creek Unit
903-395-3100

Daingerfield

Daingerfield State Park
903-645-2921

Deer Park

Battleship Texas State Historical
    Park
In San Jacinto Battleground
    State Historical Park
281-479-2411

Del Rio

Devils River State Natural Area
210-395-2133

Denison

Eisenhower Birthplace State
    Historical Park
903-465-8908

Eisenhower State Park Marina
903-465-1956

Denton

Ray Roberts Lake State Park
817-686-2148

Edna

Lake Texana State Park
512-782-5718

El Paso

Franklin Mountains State Park
915-566-6441
Hueco Tanks State Historical
Park
Indian Pictographs
Gold Texas Conservation
Passport valid only per person
915-857-1135

Magoffin Home State Historical
Park
915-533-5147

Eustace

Purtis Creek State Park
903-425-2332

Fairfield

Fairfield Lake State Park
903-389-4514

Fort Davis

Davis Mountains State Park
915-426-3337

Indian Lodge State Park
915-426-3254

Fort McKavett

Fort McKavett State Historical
Park
915-396-2358

Fort Worth

Eagle Mountain Lake State Park
817-869-7959

Fredericksburg

Admiral Nimitz Museum and
Historical Center
Japanese Garden of Peace,
History Walk of the Pacific
War
210-997-4379

Enchanted Rock State Natural
Area
915-247-3903

Fulton

Copano Bay Fishing Pier
512-729-8633

Fulton Mansion State Historical
Park
Charge for tours only
512-729-0386

Galveston

Galveston Island State Park
Summer Dramas
409-737-1222

Glen Rose

Dinosaur Valley State Park
817-897-4588

Goliad

Fannin Battleground State
Historical Park
512-645-2020

Goliad State Historical Park
Spanish Mission and General
Ignacio Zaragoza's Birthplace
512-645-3405

Granbury

Acton State Historical Park
Burial Site of Davy Crockett's Wife
817-645-4215

Greenville

Lake Rita Blanca State Park
806-488-2227

Groesbeck

Old Fort Parker State Historical
   Park
Charge for tours only
817-729-5253

Houston

Sheldon Lake State Park &
   Wildlife Management Area
281-456-9350

Huntsville

Huntsville State Park
409-295-5644

Jacksboro

Fort Richardson State Historical
   Park
817-567-3506

Jasper

Martin Dies, Jr., State Park
409-384-5231

Johnson City

Pedernales Falls State Park
210-868-7304

Junction

South Llano River State Park
915-446-3994

Karnack

Caddo Lake State Park
903-679-3351

Kerrville

Kerrville-Schreiner State Park
210-257-5392

La Grange

Monument Hills/Kreische
   Brewery State Historical Park
Kreische Brewery and House
   Tour
409-968-5658

La Porte

San Jacinto Battleground-
   Monument State Historical
   Park
Battleship TEXAS
281-479-2431

Lajitas

Big Bend Ranch State Park
   Complex
North of Hwy. 170
915-229-3416

Langtry

Seminole Canyon State
   Historical Park
Indian Pictographs
915-292-4464

Laredo

Lake Casa Blanca State Park
210-725-3826

Ledbetter

Lake Somerville State Park
Nails Creek-South of Lake
409-289-2392

Livingston

Lake Livingston State Park
409-365-2201

Lockhart

Lockhart State Park
512-398-3479

Lubbock

Lubbock Lake Landmark State
   Historical Park
Charge for tours only
806-765-0737

Luling

Palmetto State Park
210-672-3266

Lumberton

Village Creek State Park
409-755-7322

Marshall

Starr Family State Historical Park
903-935-3044

Mathis

Lake Corpus Christi State Park
512-547-2635

Meridian

Meridian State Park
817-435-2536

Mexia

Confederate Reunion Grounds
   State Historical Park
817-562-5751

Fort Parker State Park
817-562-5751

Mineral Wells

Lake Mineral Wells State Park
817-328-1171

Mission

Bentsen-Rio Grande Valley State
   Park
210-585-1107

Monahans

Monahans Sandhills State Park
915-943-2092

Moody

Mother Neff State Park
817-853-2389

Mount Pleasant

Lake Bob Sandlin State Park
903-572-5531

New Caney

Lake Houston State Park
281-354-6881

Ozona

Fort Lancaster State Historical
Park
Charge for tours only
915-836-4391

Palestine

Rusk/Palestine State Park
903-683-5126

Paris

Sam Bell Maxey House State
Historical Park
Charge for tours only
903-785-5716

Point Comfort

Port Lavaca Fishing Pier
512-552-5311

Port Aransas

Mustang Island State Park
512-749-5246

Port Arthur

Sea Rim State Park
409-971-2559

Port Isabel

Port Isabel Lighthouse State
Historical Park
Charge for tours only
210-943-1172

Port O'Connor

Matagorda Island State Park
512-983-2215

Presidio

Chinati Mountains State Park
Big Bend Ranch Complex
915-229-3416

Fort Leaton State Historical Park
Charge for tours only
915-229-3613

Quanah

Copper Breaks State Park
817-839-4331

Quitaque

Caprock Canyons State Park
806-455-1492

Quitman

Governor Hogg Shrine State
Historical Park
Honeymoon Cottage and
Stinson Home
Charge for tours only
903-763-2701

Richmond

Brazos Bend State Park
409-553-5101

Rockport

Goose Island State Park
512-729-2858

Rocksprings

Devil's Sinkhole State Natural
Area
210-563-2342

Rusk

Jim Hogg State Historical Park
903-683-4850

Rusk/Palestine State Park
903-683-5126
Texas State Railroad State
    Historical Park
Contact park for schedule of
    runs: 800-442-8951
903-683-2561

Sabine Pass

Sabine Pass Battleground State
    Historical Park
409-971-2451

San Angelo

San Angelo State Park
915-949-4757

San Antonio

Casa Navarro State Historical Park
210-226-4801

Government Canyon State
    Natural Area
210-219-8821

San Felipe

Stephen F. Austin State
    Historical Park
409-885-3613

San Marcos

John J. Stokes San Marcos River
    State Park
512-912-7100

San Patricio

Lipantitlan State Historical Park
512-547-2635

Seguin

Sebastopol State Park
Charge for tours only
210-379-4833

Smithville

Buescher State Park
512-237-2241

Somerville

Lake Somerville State Park
Birch Creek–North of Lake
409-535-7763

South Sulphur

Cooper Lake State Park
South Sulphur Unit
903-945-5256

Stonewall

Lyndon B. Johnson State
    Historical Park
210-644-2252

Tatum

Martin Creek Lake State Park
903-836-4336

Terlingua

Big Bend Ranch State Park
    Complex

Barton Warnock Environmental
    Education Center
915-424-3327

Three Rivers

Choke Canyon State Park
South Shore Unit
512-786-3538

Tyler

Camp Ford State Historical Park
903-595-2938

Tyler State Park
903-597-5338

Vanderpool

Lost Maples State Natural Area
210-966-3413

Washington

Washington-on-the-Brazos State
    Historical Park
Anson Jones Home and
    Independence Hall
Charge for tours only
409-878-2214

Weches

Mission Tejas State Historical
    Park
409-687-2394

West Columbia

Varner-Hogg State Historical
    Park
Plantation House Museum
Charge for tours only
409-345-4656

Whitney

Lake Whitney State Park
Airstrip available
817-694-3793

Wichita Falls

Lake Arrowhead State Park
817-528-2211

Willis Point

Lake Tawakoni State Park
903-595-2938

Zapata

Falcon State Park
210-848-5327

Cruises, Bus, and Rail Tours

CAPITAL CRUISES

Located at the Hyatt Regency in Austin, Capital Cruises offers dinner cruises and excursions for groups of two to sixty (or more with multiple boats). They also offer hourly rentals of pedal boats, canoes, kayaks, and electric boats.

Capital Cruises offers a senior discount on most of their services. To reserve your cruise or outing, call them with your credit card number, 50% cash or check deposit, or a purchase order number to bill against.

AGE: 60
DISCOUNT: 10% off, except Romantic Cruise
PHONE: 512-480-9264

Capital Cruises offers the following services:

- Romantic Dinner Cruises (including the Honeymoon Bat Watching Cruise—no kidding!) $32–$60 per person plus tax and gratuity.
- Group Dinner Cruise with Hyatt Fajitas, BBQ, or Chicken Pasta, $20–$50 (per person plus tax, gratuity, alcohol). Senior discount is 10%.

- Bat Watching Excursions and Public Sightseeing Tours cost to seniors is $6.50.
- Party Boat Cruises (Bring your own food and drink; no outside caterers please) $6.50–$15 (per person plus tax and gratuity). Senior discount is 10%.

LONE STAR RIVER BOAT*

Enjoy a one-and-one-half-hour cruise around Town Lake in Austin on a pleasant afternoon or moonlit night.

AGE:	60
DISCOUNT:	$2 off
COST:	$7 for seniors (Wednesdays half-price fares)
PHONE:	512-327-1388

Passengers will board on the south shore between the Congress Avenue and South First Street bridges. Boarding is 30 minutes prior to departure, and Lone Star River Boat observes the following schedule:

March–May

Saturday and Sunday: 3:00 p.m.

June–August

Tuesday–Sunday: 5:30 p.m.
Friday Moonlight Cruise: 10:30 p.m.

September–October

Saturday and Sunday: 3:00 p.m.

VANISHING TEXAS RIVER CRUISE**

The rugged Colorado River is the backdrop for this remarkable river cruise. In the comfort of their 70-foot, 200-passenger

---

* (Source: *Lone Star River Boat,* Lone Star River Boat, Inc.)
** (Source: *Vanishing Texas River Cruise,* Vanishing Texas River Cruise, Inc.)

cruise boat, you'll experience the natural beauty of the Colorado complete with spectacular waterfalls and sheer cliffs.

AGE: 60
COST: $13 for seniors
PHONE: 512-756-6986

The Texas Eagle II has an enclosed all-weather deck plus two observation decks, and they operate year-round. Reservations are recommended for this two-and-one-half-hour cruise. Enjoy a Captain's box lunch or bring your own picnic lunch.

CRUISE SHIPS

Cruise lines operating out of Texas ports include Norwegian Cruise Line (NCL) sailing from the Port of Houston and Royal Olympic Cruise Line sailing from Galveston. While neither of these cruise lines offers senior discounts, per se, they both offer attractive group discounts.

PHONE: Norwegian Cruise Line: 800-327-7030
        Royal Olympic Cruise Line: 800-445-6400

There once were evening gambling cruise ships sailing from Galveston, but these have been discontinued.

BUS TOURS

FUN TIME TOURS

Fun Time Tours is a charter and tour company in Corpus Christi, Texas.

AGE: 66 and up
DISCOUNT: 10%
COST: Ranges from $11.25–$20.25
              (including discount)
PHONE: 512-289-7965

City Tour

- Bayfront and Port
- Ocean Drive Mansions
- Museums
- Texas State Aquarium
- Historical Sites
- Heritage Park
- USS Lexington

Loop Tour

- Ferry to Port Aransas
- Padre Island Park
- Visit Conn Brown Harbor

Casino Tours (Free)

- Casino Tours—10 hours of gambling guaranteed
- Monday–Tuesday and Saturday–Sunday departures
  21 years or older and groups welcome

GRAY LINE TOURS*

Gray Line Tours operates world-wide and in many cities in Texas. They provide sightseeing and group day tours.

AGE:	60 (50 with AARP card)
DISCOUNT:	$3
HONORS:	AARP
COST:	Tours range from $17–$29 (including discount)

Austin Highlights Tour 800-950-8285

- Texas State Capitol
- 130-year-old Governor's Mansion
- The University of Texas Campus (UT Tower and Darrell K. Royal Memorial Stadium)

---

* (Sources: *See the Heart of Texas - Austin* and *Dallas Sightseeing Tours; San Antonio Gray Line Tour,* Gray Line, Inc.)

- Lyndon B. Johnson Presidential Library
- Treaty Oak
- Barton Springs
- Zilker Park Nature Gardens
- Sixth Street—Austin's Musical Heartbeat
- Historic Austin Neighborhoods

Dallas City Tour #1 214-630-1000

- Kennedy Memorial
- Union Station
- Convention Center
- City Hall
- Old City Park (stop)
- Highland Park Area
- Fair Park
- Belo Mansion
- Southern Methodist University
- Pioneer Cemetery
- Neiman Marcus
- Reunion Arena
- Myerson Symphony
- Old Red Court House
- Farmers Market
- West End Market
- Uptown McKinney
- Dallas Museum of Art

J.F.K. Historical Tour #2

This tour highlights the events of that fateful day in Dallas in November 1963 and includes a tour of the West End Historical District:

- Lee Oswald Rooming House
- Texas Theater
- Parkland Hospital
- Dallas Police Department
- Love Field
- Kennedy Motorcade Route
- Trademart
- Jack Ruby Apartment
- Site of Tippit Killing
- 214 Neely Street
- Dealey Plaza
- Walking Tour

South Fork Ranch #3

Experience some of the *Dallas* legend with longhorns, horses, and the Ewing Mansion.

Dallas Then and Now

This tour is a combination of Tours #1 and #2 at a reduced cost with an independent half-hour lunch and shopping break. You may dine at either Uptown McKinney (includes the Hard Rock Cafe) and take a ride on the McKinney Avenue Trolley or visit the West End Market Place with over 100 merchants.

Best of "Big D" #4

A combination of Tours #1 and #3 at a reduced cost with a half-hour independent lunch break at one of the West End's 80 restaurants.

The Alamo and Spanish Colonial Missions #1 San Antonio 800-472-9546

- Mission San Jose
- Mission Espada
- San Fernando Cathedral
- The Alamo
- San Juan Capistrano
- Mission Concepcion
- La Villita

San Antonio Sampler #2

- Brackenridge Park
- San Antonio Gardens
- El Mercado Shopping
- Lone Star Brewery
- San Antonio Zoo
- Fort Sam Houston
- King William Historic District
- Institute of Texan Cultures

Alamo City Grand Tour #3

Combination of Tours #1 and #2 including a one-hour lunch on the Riverwalk and a river barge cruise down the San Antonio River.

Texas Hill Country Escape #4

- Shopping in Fredericksburg
- Admiral Nimitz Museum
- LBJ Ranch & Birthplace
- Lukenbach

GREYHOUND

Greyhound offers bus service to many Texas locations. There may be deeper seasonal or advance purchase discounts available.

AGE: 55 and up
DISCOUNT: 10%
PHONE: 800-231-2222
  (En Español: 800-531-5332)

KERRVILLE BUS & TOUR CO.

Kerrville Bus & Tour Company offers a variety of services. Ask about the deepest discounts available because discounts for advance purchase of your tickets may be better than your senior discount.

AGE: 55 and older
DISCOUNT: 5–15% on different services

The Kerrville Bus & Tour Company offers the following:

- Bus service to many Texas locations (800-335-3722)
- Deluxe motorcoach transportation for private use by groups out of Austin, Dallas/Fort Worth, Houston, and San Antonio (800-256-4723)
- Kerrville Tours—Crown Escorted Vacations—tours departing from North, East, Central, and South Texas to the USA and Canada (800-442-8705)

CITY BUS SERVICE

Metropolitan Transit Authorities (MTAs) operate in the state's seven largest cities and are under the guidance of the Texas Department of Transportation.

INTERNET: http://www.dot.state.tx.us
Phone: 800-452-9292

CAPITAL METROPOLITAN TRANSPORTATION AUTHORITY—AUSTIN

Austin seniors who are 65 and better ride free on the Capital Metro Easy Rider Program by showing their photo ID or driver's license.

Senior Group Transportation Program. Capital Metro, in Austin, will provide free transportation for groups of 20 or more seniors Monday-Friday from 10 a.m.—2 p.m. and after 7 p.m. They will provide this same service anytime on the weekends. This offer is subject to availability of buses. Call the toll-free number below to make reservations for your next group outing to the movies, shopping, or other excursion.

Special Transit Service (STS). Capital Metro also offers Austinites a valuable service for the disabled and mobility impaired called the Special Transit Service. This (almost free) transportation service can make a profound difference in the lives of persons with disabilities because transportation makes opportunities possible. This service is not based on financial need, only disability and mobility impairment.

The cost is only 60 cents each way for transportation anywhere you need to go in a 505-square-mile service area—grocery store, shopping, doctor appointment, visit to a friend. You can also purchase a 10-ride ticket book or a monthly pass for $15 at H.E.B. grocery stores.

With a fleet of 45 vans and 32 sedans, STS ridership in 1996 totaled 2,000 daily trips to Austin, Cedar Park, Jonestown, Lago Vista, Leander, Manor, Pflugerville, and San Leana.

Call Capital Metro and they'll mail you a four-page application where you'll detail your disability or impairment. There's also a section for your physician to verify your disability. Once approved, call and make reservations up to eight days in advance (minimum, the day before).

PHONE:	800-474-1201
	512-389-7480 (STS Information)
	512-389-7583 (Easy Rider Program)

CORPUS CHRISTI REGIONAL TRANSPORTATION AUTHORITY

Corpus Christi's city bus service, known as "The B," offers seniors who are 60 or better a discount. Seniors can purchase a monthly pass for $11, regularly priced at $20, that allows them unlimited bus use. For casual bus riders, seniors pay a dime per ride between 9 a.m. and 3 p.m. (20 cents beyond these hours) instead of the usual 50 cents.

| AGE: | 60 |
| PHONE: | 512-883-2287 |

DALLAS AREA RAPID TRANSIT—DART (DALLAS)

Seniors ride for 50 cents on Dallas city buses or they can buy a monthly pass for $10 and have unlimited rides.

| AGE: | 65 |
| PHONE: | 214-749-3278 |

FORT WORTH TRANSIT AUTHORITY

Seniors 65 or over can ride "The T" for 40 cents instead of the usual 80 cents. They also have the option of buying a $16 monthly pass for unlimited bus use. They'll need to pay $2 to purchase a senior ID card.

| AGE: | 65 |
| PHONE: | 817-870-6221 |

METROPOLITAN TRANSIT AUTHORITY OF HARRIS COUNTY—HOUSTON

Houston seniors ride for half fare on Houston city buses. They can get an annual Metro ID Senior Card for $52 at one of four locations: two in the downtown area, one at the Medical Center, and one in Sharpstown Mall.

AGE: 62
PHONE: 713-739-4831

SUN METRO—EL PASO

El Paso seniors 65 or better can enjoy discounted bus service with the purchase of a $2.50 identification card. They'll ride buses for 30 cents instead of $1 per ride. They also have the option of purchasing an unlimited-use pass for $10 a month.

VIA—SAN ANTONIO

VIA offers seniors in San Antonio half-fare rides when they have a Senior Citizen ID card or show proof of age. The ID card may be obtained for free at 112 Soledad with proof of age.

AGE: 62
PHONE: 210-227-5371

RAIL TOURS

AMTRAK—TEXAS EAGLE*

If you've ever wanted to cross America by train, Amtrak is the way. Rail travel offers you a window-seat view to the incredible beauty of this country. With the precarious future of Amtrak, you may not want to put this off.

The Texas Eagle "takes you to the unique attractions and big-city excitement of Chicago, St. Louis, and Dallas-Fort Worth . . . the new casinos to Bossier City and Shreveport (conveniently accessible from Marshall and Longview) . . . the down-home country entertainment of Austin . . . San Antonio, home to the contemporary pleasures of Paseo del

---

* (Source: *1996 Amtrak Travel Planner,* Amtrak)

Rio (the River Walk) and the ancient walls of the Alamo . . . and more."

When you call their toll-free number, ask about all their discounts. Ask about their flat rate All Aboard America fare for travel within a region or adjoining region (this is a great deal), and ask them to mail you a free *Amtrak Travel Planner.*

AGE: 62 or disabled
DISCOUNT: 10% (not on sleeper cars)
PHONE: 800-USA-RAIL

Amtrak provides service to the following Texas cities:

- Alpine
- Cleburne
- Marshall
- San Antonio
- San Marcos
- Temple

- Austin
- Dallas
- Mineola
- Sanderson
- Taylor
- Texarkana

HILL COUNTRY FLYER*

All aboard to ride a steam train through the Hill Country! You'll experience the scenic views of Austin's northwest edge and travel deep into the heart of the Hill Country through 33 miles of Texas history.

You'll travel from Cedar Park through canyons, over rivers, and down valleys dotted with flowers, fauna, deer, longhorns, and emus. You'll stop in historic Burnet, with time for a leisurely lunch and shopping for gifts or antiques, before leaving for the return trip.

* (Source: *Ride the Steam Train Through the Hill Country,* The Austin & Texas Central Railroad)

If you decide to stay overnight in Burnet, you're only minutes away from three inviting Central Texas Highland Lakes, the Vanishing Texas River Cruise (see Cruises for more information), several wineries, Longhorn Cavern, and Enchanted Rock.

AGE:	62
DISCOUNT:	10%
COST:	$21.60 for seniors or $34.20 for air-conditioned lounge cars
PHONE:	512-477-8468

Call the Austin Steam Train Association and ask them to mail you a brochure about the Hill Country Flyer for all the details.

Free Stuff and Other Senior Discounts

FREE STUFF ON YOUR BIRTHDAY

BIRTHDAY CAKE

Most restaurants will help you celebrate your birthday with a free piece of birthday cake, so call your favorite restaurant and see what their birthday policy is. At the Macaroni Grill restaurants, they'll even give you a free birthday cake after your dinner there! Check your phone directory for their location near you. Also, refer to the birthday special for the Mesa Hills Cafe in Restaurants and Fast Food, if you're celebrating your birthday in Austin.

CAR WASH

Many car wash businesses will give you a free car wash on your birthday. Give them a call. Most Genie Car Wash franchises in the state offer this birthday service. They're currently located in Austin, Hewitt, and Waco.

GREETINGS FROM THE GOVERNOR'S MANSION

If you would like the governor of Texas to send a personal birthday card to a senior (no age requirement), send the name, address, and date of birth to:

The Governor's Correspondence Division
P. O. Box 12428
Austin, TX 78711

It's a good idea to mail your request at least two weeks in advance. If you need the governor for anything else:

PHONE: 800-843-5789 (Austin 512-463-1782)
INTERNET: http://www.governor.state.tx.us

GREETINGS FROM THE WHITE HOUSE

If you would like the President of the United States to send a personal birthday card to a senior 80 years or better, send the name, address, and date of birth to:

The Greetings Office, Room 39
The White House
Washington, D.C. 20500

It's a good idea to mail your request four weeks or more in advance. The President will also send greetings to commemorate a 50th (or over) wedding anniversary, but they must be 50 consecutive years of marriage!

If you need the President, Vice President, or First Lady for anything else:

PHONE: 202-451-1414
FAX: 202-456-2461
INTERNET: president@whitehouse.gov (e-mail)
             vice.president@whitehouse.gov (e-mail)
             first.lady@whitehouse.gov (e-mail)

Free Travel Information

Convention and Visitors Bureaus and Chambers of Commerce

All convention and visitors bureaus will mail you free travel information when you phone or write your request. The following list of Texas convention and visitors bureaus and chambers of commerce includes examples of the free information available.

Austin Convention and Visitors Bureau

Before you travel to Austin, the "Live Music Capital of the World," call the Austin Convention and Visitors Bureau at 800-926-2282 and they'll send:

- Calendar of Events
- Guided Walking Tour Flyer
- Austin Experience Visitors Guide

Corpus Christi Area Convention & Visitors Bureau

Corpus Christi, whose natives refer to their city as "Texas with a Tropical Twist," especially loves "winter Texans." They will happily mail the following when you call 800-678-6232:

- Beach and Bay Guide
- Corpus Christi accommodations
- Area Events and Festival Calendar
- Thick envelope filled with coupons

Dallas Convention & Visitors Bureau

You won't miss a thing in Big "D" if you contact their convention bureau at 800-752-9222 and have them mail you a visitor's packet. It includes:

- Dallas Official Visitor's Guide
- Hotel Weekend Package Guide
- Dallas Calendar of Events and Fun Things To Do
- Dallas illustrated map
- *Dallas Today* brochure

GALVESTON ISLAND CONVENTION AND VISITORS BUREAU

Call 800-351-4237 to receive the following free information:

- Galveston Island attractions
- Galveston Island Accommodations Guide
- Galveston Island Calendar of Events
- Galveston Island Money Saving Coupons

GREATER HOUSTON CONVENTION AND VISITORS BUREAU

Call 800-4-HOUSTON for hotel reservation information and 800-231-7799 to receive the following free information:

- Official Guide to Houston—The Real Texas
- 100 Highlights
- Houston's Multicultural Activities and Attractions
- Houston Passport ("$1,000 Free, Prize Giveaways")

SAN ANTONIO CONVENTION AND VISITORS BUREAU

When you call their toll-free number at 800-447-3372, they'll mail you the following brochures:

- San Antonio 1996 Lodging Guide
- San Antonio Attractions, Hotels and Restaurants Guide with "over $2,700 savings" in coupons
- Pure San Antonio

DEPARTMENT OF PUBLIC TRANSPORTATION INFORMATION

Receive any of the following (that you need) when you call Texas Travel Information at 800-888-8839 or the State Department of Public Transportation at 800-452-9292:

- Texas State Travel Guide
- Texas Accommodations Guide
- Official Texas Travel Map
- Campground Guide
- Calendar of Events for the Upcoming Quarter

Especially impressive is the glossy, full-color 272-page *Texas State Travel Guide*. It's beautiful and loaded with great information. The Texas Accommodations Guide lists inns, hotels, motels, and bed and breakfasts by city. Amenities are indicated for each accommodation and one of these notations regarding its location:

- Downtown
- Near Airport
- On the Beach
- Suburban
- Freeway
- Resort Area

The following is a complete list of Texas convention and visitors bureaus and chambers of commerce.*

Abilene Convention & Visitors Council

800-727-7704

Alice Chamber of Commerce

512-664-3454

Alvin-Manvel Chamber of Commerce

281-331-3944

Amarillo Convention & Visitors Council

806-374-1497
800-692-1338

* (Source: Internet http://www.eventplanner.com/cptx.htm)
© 1995 Interactive Marketing Technologies.

Aransas Pass Chamber of Commerce

512-758-2750

Arlington Convention & Visitors Bureau

817-640-0252
800-342-4305

Athens Convention & Visitors Department

903-675-5181

Austin Convention & Visitors Bureau

512-478-0098
800-926-2282

Bandera Convention & Visitors Bureau

210-796-3045
800-364-3833

Beaumont Convention & Visitors Bureau

409-880-3749
800-392-4401

Big Spring Area Convention & Visitors Bureau

915-263-7641

Boerne Chamber of Commerce

210-249-8000

Borger Chamber of Commerce

806-274-2211

Brady Convention & Visitors Bureau

915-597-3491

Brownsville Convention & Visitors Bureau

210-546-3721
800-626-2639

Brownwood Chamber of Commerce

915-646-9535

Bryan-College Station Convention & Visitors Bureau

409-260-9898
800-777-8292

Canton Chamber of Commerce

903-567-2991

Clear Lake NASA Area Convention & Visitors Bureau

713-488-7676

Conroe Visitor & Convention Bureau

409-756-6644

Corpus Christi Area Convention & Tourist Bureau

512-882-5603
800-678-6232

Dallas Convention & Visitors Bureau

214-746-6600
800-752-9222

Del Rio Chamber of Commerce

210-775-3551

Denton Convention & Visitors Bureau

817-382-7895

El Paso Convention & Visitors Bureau

915-534-0653
800-351-6024

Ennis Convention & Visitors Bureau

214-875-2625

Farmers Branch Development/Tourism

214-919-2510
800-272-6249

Fort Worth Convention & Visitors Bureau

817-336-8791
800-433-5747

Fredericksburg Convention & Visitors Bureau

210-997-6523

Gainesville Area Chamber of Commerce

817-665-2831

Galveston Convention & Visitors Bureau

409-763-4311
800-351-4237

Garland Convention & Visitors Bureau

214-205-2749

Georgetown Convention & Visitors Bureau

512-930-3545
800-436-8696

Granbury Convention & Visitors Bureau

817-573-5548
800-950-2212

Grand Prairie Convention & Visitors Bureau

214-264-1558

Grapevine Convention & Visitors Bureau

817-481-0454
800-457-6338

Greenville Convention & Visitors Bureau

903-455-1510

Harlingen Chamber of Commerce

210-423-5440
800-531-7346

Henderson Tourist Development

903-657-5528

Hillsboro Convention & Visitors Bureau

817-582-2481

Houston Convention & Visitors Bureau

713-227-3100
800-231-7799

Huntsville Visitor & Convention Bureau

409-295-8113
800-289-0389

Irving Convention & Visitors Bureau

214-252-7476
800-247-8464

Johnson City Chamber of Commerce

210-868-7684

Kerrville Convention & Visitors Bureau

210-792-3535
800-221-7958

Killeen Visitors & Convention Bureau

817-526-9551
800-869-8265

Kingsville Visitor Center

512-592-8516
800-333-5032

La Grange Area Chamber of Commerce

409-968-5756

City of Laredo Convention & Visitors Bureau

210-712-1230
800-361-3360

Lewisville Visitors Bureau

214-436-9571

Llano County Chamber of Commerce

915-247-5354

Longview Convention & Visitors Bureau

903-753-3281
800-833-5282

Lubbock Visitors & Convention Bureau

806-763-4666
800-692-4035

Lufkin Convention & Visitors Bureau

409-634-6305

McAllen Convention &
Visitors Bureau

210-682-2871

McKinney Chamber of
Commerce

214-542-0163

Marshall Visitor
Development Division

903-935-7868

Mesquite Tourism,
Convention & Promotion
Division

214-285-0211

Midland Convention &
Visitors Bureau

915-683-3381
800-624-6435

Mineral Wells Chamber of
Commerce

817-325-2557
800-252-6989

Mt. Pleasant & Titus
County Chamber of
Commerce

903-572-8567

Nacogdoches Tourist &
Convention Department

409-564-7351

New Braunfels Convention
& Visitors Bureau

210-625-2385
800-572-2626

Odessa Convention &
Visitors Bureau

915-332-9111
800-583-6400

Orange Area Chamber of
Commerce

409-883-3536
800-528-4906

Palestine Convention &
Visitors Bureau

903-729-6066

Paris Visitors and
Convention Committee

903-784-2501

Pecos Department of
Tourism & General
Development

915-445-2406

Plainview Chamber of
Commerce

806-296-7431

Plano Convention &
Visitors Bureau

214-578-7112

Port Aransas Chamber of
Commerce

512-749-5919
800-452-6278

Port Arthur Convention & Visitors Bureau
409-985-7822
800-235-7822

Richardson Chamber of Commerce
214-234-4141

Rockport-Fulton Area Chamber of Commerce
512-729-6445

Round Rock Convention & Visitors Bureau
512-255-5805

San Angelo Convention & Visitors Bureau
915-653-3162
800-375-1206

San Antonio Convention & Visitors Bureau
210-270-8700
800-447-3372

San Marcos Convention & Visitors Bureau
512-396-2495
800-782-7653

Seguin Visitor & Convention Department
210-379-6382

Sherman Convention & Visitors Bureau
903-893-1184

Snyder Chamber of Commerce
915-761-3005

Sonora Chamber of Commerce
915-387-2880

South Padre Island Tourist Bureau
210-761-6433
800-343-2368

Southern Brazoria County Convention & Visitors Bureau
409-265-2508
800-938-4853

Temple Convention & Visitors Bureau
817-770-5720

Texarkana Chamber of Commerce
903-792-7191

Tyler Convention & Visitors Council
903-592-1661
800-235-5712

Uvalde Convention & Visitors Bureau
210-278-4115

Van Horn Convention
Center & Visitors Bureau

915-283-2682

Victoria Convention &
Visitors Bureau

512-573-5277

Waco Convention &
Visitors Bureau

817-753-3621
800-922-6386

Washington County
Convention & Visitors
Bureau

409-836-3695

Waxahachie Convention &
Visitors Bureau

214-937-2390

Weatherford
Chamber/Visitors Center

817-594-3801

West Columbia Chamber of
Commerce

409-345-3921

Wichita Falls Convention &
Visitors Bureau

817-723-9988
800-799-6732

DISCOUNTS AT SCHOOL DISTRICTS

A survey of the larger school districts around the state found that many of them offer senior discounts on athletic events, high school plays, and other school performances. Some programs are only for retired district employees, and some include all seniors living in their school district.

AMARILLO INDEPENDENT SCHOOL DISTRICT

PROGRAM: Gold Club
ELIGIBLE: District retirees and all seniors living
             in the district
AGE: 65
DISCOUNT: Free admission to any regular season school
             athletic contest (excluding playoff games);
             free admission to any AISD-sponsored per-
             formance by the district's students; free
             breakfast or lunch in any school cafeteria.
PHONE: 806-354-4200

AUSTIN INDEPENDENT SCHOOL DISTRICT

PROGRAM: Proud to be a Senior
ELIGIBLE: District retirees and all seniors living
                     in the district
AGE: 55
DISCOUNT: Free or discounted attendance at all events
PHONE: 512-414-2414

DALLAS INDEPENDENT SCHOOL DISTRICT

PROGRAM: Golden Age Card
ELIGIBLE: Retired employees of the Dallas
                     school district
AGE: Any retiree
DISCOUNT: Free attendance at athletic events and
                     cultural performances performed by the
                     district's students
PHONE: 214-989-8000

EANES INDEPENDENT SCHOOL DISTRICT

PROGRAM: Gold Star Club
ELIGIBLE: District retirees and all seniors living
                     in the district
AGE: 65
DISCOUNT: Free admission to any Westlake High
                     School athletic contest played at Westlake
                     (excluding playoff games); ten-dollar
                     discount on the price of EISD Community
                     Education classes; free admission to any
                     EISD-sponsored performance by the
                     district's students
PHONE: 512-329-3613

EL PASO INDEPENDENT SCHOOL DISTRICT

PROGRAM: Senior Discount
ELIGIBLE: Retired employees of the El Paso school
                    district
AGE: Any retiree
DISCOUNT: Free attendance at regular season athletic
                    events and cultural performances performed
                    by the district's students
PHONE: 915-779-3781

HOUSTON INDEPENDENT SCHOOL DISTRICT

PROGRAM: Golden Age Card
ELIGIBLE: Retired employees of the Houston
                    school district
AGE: Any retiree
DISCOUNT: Free lifetime pass to regular season athletic
                    events and cultural performances performed
                    by the district's students
PHONE: 713-892-6121

MISCELLANEOUS

WHITE HOUSE PHOTO TOUR BOOK*

Write to the White House, and in about 12 weeks they'll mail you a color photo tour book of the White House for free! They'll also include a separate photograph of the President if you ask.

President's Correspondence
The White House
Washington, D.C. 20500

---

* (Source: Lesko, M. with Martello, M. A., *Free Stuff for Seniors*, Kensington, MD: Information USA, Inc., 1995, pp. 568–569.)

Freebies Magazine/Senior Offer

Write to *Freebies* magazine and get a discounted one-year (five issues) subscription for $4.95.

Freebies Senior Offer
1135 Eugenia Place
P. O. Box 5025
Carpenteria, Ca. 93014

MAIL BOXES ETC.

Mail Boxes Etc. stores are individually owned, and I only found one giving a senior discount. Seniors who visit Mail Boxes Etc. in the Westlake area near Austin will receive this discount.

AGE:	60
DISCOUNT:	$2 off UPS shipments over $10
ADDRESS:	3267 Bee Caves Rd., Ste. 107
	Austin
PHONE:	512-328-7933

This Mail Boxes Etc. also provides:

- Mail and overnight shipments
- Office and shipping supplies and full service packaging
- Copy and fax services (discount card for "frequent faxers")
- Mail box rental
- Notary

SENIOROPTIONS WEB SITE

If you're an Internet user, check out the numerous "senior" Web sites (a.k.a. home pages) dedicated to senior citizens. There's a lot of good information on the World Wide Web (Internet), and it's free. If you're not connected at home or work, many public libraries now offer free connection to the Internet (also known as the Information Super Highway) and will assist you in your search. Just do a search on the keywords "senior+Texas+discounts," and you'll be amazed at how much information is available! An example of a Web site is called SeniorOptions.

PHONE: 512-345-2646 (Senior Business
                       Concerns, Inc.)
INTERNET: http://www.senioroptions.com

SeniorOptions is a public service Internet site (Web page) providing comprehensive, yet local (city or county), directories identifying the facilities, agencies, firms, practices, and businesses who help older adults throughout the United States. Typical users of the SeniorOptions site are:

- Older adults shopping for services, housing, or products
- Adult children responsible for the care of an older adult
- Attorneys, accountants, financial planners, and other professionals needing to refer clients for services outside their areas of expertise or geographic region
- Anyone looking for senior housing options anywhere in the United States.

The directories are organized by service categories. Internet users are not charged for access to these directories and may even print them for later use. Likewise, providers are not charged to be listed in the directories.

LIST OF FREE STUFF IN THIS BOOK

Groceries and Specialty Food

GROCERY STORES

FOOD KING

When you shop at your Food King grocery store in Dickinson, Galveston, and Texas City, you'll receive 5% off the purchase price up to a $50 purchase.

AGE: 60
DISCOUNT: 5% off purchase price (up to a $50 purchase) on Wednesdays only

KROGER FOOD STORES

Seniors, age 59 and better, can enjoy free coffee while they do their grocery shopping at their local Kroger Store. The store will also waive fees for check cashing and utility payments for seniors, and allow them to purchase one over the limit on limited items. During Kroger's annual "turkey buck" promotion, seniors get one turkey buck for each $20 purchase instead of the usual $30 purchase for other customers.

RANDALLS, SIMON DAVID STORE, AND TOM THUMB

The "remarkable" Randalls stores, along with the Tom Thumb stores and the Simon David store in Austin are owned by the

Tom Thumb Co. in Houston. These stores share the distinction of having the best senior program among the grocery stores in Texas. Each of these stores offers the following benefits to seniors 60 and up:

- Free coffee
- Fees waived for check cashing and utility payments
- No limit on advertised specials
- Electric carts
- Discounts on plates in the deli (at participating stores only)
- One Turkey Buck for every $20 purchase (instead of $30 purchase) during their annual Turkey Bucks promotion

SUN HARVEST FARMS

This food market specializes in all natural products. Have lunch in their cafe while you decide what to buy from the market, produce section, or extensive vitamin supplement/herb department.

AGE: 60
DISCOUNT: 10% off vitamin supplements on Monday only

You'll find Sun Harvest Farms stores in Austin, Corpus Christi, El Paso, McAllen, and San Antonio

WHEATSVILLE FOOD CO-OP

You'll find natural and organic groceries at this Austin grocery store. They also have a deli, dairy and frozen foods, and bulk groceries.

AGE: 62
DISCOUNT: Free membership for seniors
PHONE: 512-478-2667

Free membership saves seniors the $10 per year membership fee ($70/lifetime). Members are not charged the 7% surcharge on purchases nonmembers are charged.

BAKERIES

CHESAPEAKE BAGEL BAKERY*

With three locations and growing, Chesapeake Bagel Bakery serves breakfast, lunch, and dinner. They also offer an espresso bar and shaded outdoor patio at their Austin 6th Street location.

AGE: 50 (Austin), 60 (Houston)
DISCOUNT: 10%
ADDRESS: 601 W. 6th Street
Austin
512-473-3772

3421 William Cannon
Austin
512-891-0855

5525 Westland
Houston
713-669-9985

The Chesapeake Bagel Bakery company was founded in 1981 and is the nation's oldest "full-scratch" bagel bakery franchise. Their bagels are kettle-boiled and stone-hearth baked.

You can order bagel deli sandwiches, hot sandwiches (open face), specialty sandwiches, soups, salads, desserts, and pastries. They also provide catering for corporate accounts with platters and boxed lunches.

---

* (Source: *Catering to Business*, Chesapeake Bagel Bakery)

Entenmanns-Oroweat Bakery Outlets

For yummy baked goods, the Entenmanns-Oroweat Bakery out-
lets offer a discount to seniors 60 and better every Monday and
Thursday. Some locations offer senior discounts more often, so check
with the location near you. In addition to Entenmanns-Oroweat
products, they also carry Boboli and Thomas Muffins and bagels.

AGE: 60
DISCOUNT: 10% (Mention this book, and they'll give
                you a free loaf of Oroweat Bread.)

Mrs Baird's Bakeries—Thrift Stores

There are different discount policies across the Mrs Baird's
Bakeries—Thrift Stores. Most of the thrift stores in Austin offer
a 10% discount to seniors 55 and over on Thursdays. The Dallas
area stores offer a 10% discount on all purchases on Wednesdays.
In addition, the Dallas area locations offer one free item of the
store's choice with a $5 purchase. Fort Worth offers no senior
discounts at this time.

Ice Cream and Yogurt

Baskin Robbins

Most of the Baskin Robbins ice cream parlors offer a Silver
Discount Card to seniors, but a few do not offer any discount.

To receive the discount, fill out their application and you'll
receive your card in the mail. Some parlors just ask you to show
your driver's license or some form of identification with your
birth date. Please call your local Baskin Robbins to find out
about their discount program.

AGE: 55
DISCOUNT: 10%
PHONE: Silver Discount Card: 800-331-0031

Hotels

GENERAL GUIDELINES

When you're making reservations or checking in, always ask for the deepest discounts available. The hotel may be able to offer you deeper discounts than their senior or AARP rate due to availability. The weekend rates for many hotels are better than week-night rates. Most hotels do offer some type of senior discount. I've included a sample here to give you an idea of what's available.

Most hotel chains offer a free directory of their locations across the country. Call the toll-free numbers listed to have one mailed to you.

CHOICE HOTELS INTERNATIONAL*

This organization includes the following hotels:

• Sleep Inns
• Comfort Inns and Suites
• Quality Inns and Suites
• Clarion Inns, Hotels, Suites and Resorts

Seniors who are 50 and better receive a 10% discount at these hotels, year round, subject to availability. You also receive a 30% discount when you call their toll-free number and ask for the

---

* (Source: *Travel & Vacation Directory*, Choice Hotels International)

Prime Rate. Only one discount applies per stay, and covers hotels in the USA and Canada.

AGE: 50
DISCOUNT: 10–30%
HONORS: AARP
              United Airlines Silver Wings Plus
              AAA (10% discount at Sleep Inns, Comfort
              Inns and Suites, and Quality Inns and
              Suites; 20% discount at most Clarion Hotels
              and Resorts)
PHONE: 800-221-2222

HOLIDAY INN*

At participating Holiday Inns across Texas, you'll find the Alumni Travel Program for seniors 50 and better. With this free program, you'll receive a minimum of 20% discount on the single room rate and a 10% discount in their restaurants. To enroll, call the toll-free number below, and they'll enroll you over the phone or mail you an application. The discounted rooms are subject to availability. Holiday Inn also offers AARP and military discounts.

AGE: 50
DISCOUNT: 20% on rooms, 10% in restaurants
HONORS: AARP and military discounts
PHONE: Reservations: 800-HOLIDAY
              Alumni Club: 800-ALUMNI2

HYATT REGENCY HOTELS AND RESORTS**

Most Hyatt Regency locations offer seniors 25% off the full published rates subject to availability.

---

* (Source: *World Wide Directory,* Holiday Inn)
** (Source: *Hyatt Hotels & Resorts Worldwide Guide,* Hyatt Corporation)

```
AGE:        62
DISCOUNT:   25%
HONORS:     AARP
PHONE:      800-233-1234
```

MARRIOTT COURTYARD AND MARRIOTT RESIDENCE INN*

Marriott doesn't offer a senior discount, per se, but they do honor AARP memberships.

```
AGE:        50 with AARP card
DISCOUNT:   10–15%
PHONE:      Courtyard: 800-321-2211
            Residence Inn: 800-331-3131
```

MENGER HOTEL**

Designated as one of the Historic Hotels of America, you'll want to stay at the elegant Menger Hotel, or at least see it when you're in San Antonio. Built in 1859, 23 years after the fall of the Alamo, the Menger has played host to Teddy Roosevelt, the Vanderbilts, Sarah Bernhardt, Oscar Wilde, and "O. Henry." Call their toll-free number for a brochure or to make reservations.

```
AGE:        65
DISCOUNT:   Approximately 19% (depending on size of
            room, date, and availability)
HONORS:     AARP (age 50)
ADDRESS:    204 Alamo Plaza
            San Antonio
PHONE:      800-345-9285
```

---

 * (Source: *1996 Worldwide Directory*, Marriott)
** (Source: *This is Texas! Menger Hotel*, Menger Hotel)

RAMADA*

Ramada offers a discount program for seniors called Best Years for Seniors. For a $15 lifetime membership, seniors who are 60 and better get a 25% discount at most locations, dependent upon the date of your stay and room availability. Call the toll-free number to enroll.

AGE: 60
DISCOUNT: Up to 25%
HONORS: AARP, AAA, and military discounts
PHONE: Reservations: 800-2-RAMADA
                    Best Years for Seniors: 800-766-2378

When you're a member of Best Years for Seniors, you'll receive:

- 25% off standard rates (based on single or double occupancy) at over 650 participating locations
- 15 Club Points for each dollar transaction appearing on your hotel folio. Earn free hotel stays, airline tickets, merchandise, and more
- Express check-in and checkout; automatic room upgrades when available at check-in; extended checkout when requested in advance
- Toll-free customer service number, for members only
- Alamo Rent-A-Car discounts
- Discounts on cruises in the Caribbean, Hawaii, Mexico, Mediterranean, or Bahamas
- Discounts on foreign tours to Europe, Mexico, Australia, and many other locations
- Discounts on special attractions

---

* (Source: *Best Years By Ramada* and *Ramada Worldwide Directory,* Ramada)

SHONEY'S INN*

Join the Shoney's Inn Any Senior Program for free and enjoy a 15% discount off the regular room rate, subject to room availability. Call their toll-free number to enroll. This discount isn't available in their restaurants, but refer to Restaurants and Fast Food for information about senior discounts at Shoney's Restaurants.

AGE: 55
DISCOUNT: 10% discount off applicable room type
              and occupancy
HONORS: AARP and government per diem rates
PHONE: Reservations: 800-222-2222
              Any Senior Program: 800-222-2222

THE DRISKILL HOTEL**

This Historic Hotel of America is widely recognized for true Texas hospitality and is located in Austin's downtown entertainment district. Built in 1886, The Driskill Hotel has played host to dignitaries and heads of state, lobbyists, legislators, socialites, honeymooners, and filmmakers for over a century. Call their toll-free number for a brochure or reservations.

AGE: 65
DISCOUNT: 10–15% depending on availability
HONORS: AARP and AAA
ADDRESS: 6th and Brazos St.
              Austin
PHONE: 800-252-9367

* (Source: *1995 Travel and Vacation Directory,* Shoney's Inn)
** (Source: *The Driskill Austin, Texas,* The Driskill)

Legal Services and Taxes

For legal advice and referrals, contact the Legal Hotline for Older Texans at the State Bar of Texas. They'll give legal advice and referrals. Some attorneys offer services on a reduced scale based on income and some will offer senior discounts. Another source of help in this area is your local Area Agency on Aging. Please refer to Senior Organizations for the address of your nearest Area Agency on Aging.

PHONE: Legal Hotline for Older Adults:
           800-622-2520

National Academy of Elder Law Attorneys, Inc. (NAELA)

An additional resource for locating attorneys who specialize in elder law is the NAELA located in Tucson, Arizona. Attorneys who specialize in elder law differ from other lawyers because they focus on the needs of a particular population, not a certain group of laws. They specialize in estate and retirement planning and need knowledge of medical care, nursing homes, and ways in which a person ages.

According to the NAELA, these are some questions one should ask when choosing an attorney who specializes in elder law:

- How long has the lawyer been specializing in elder law?
- How much of the lawyer's practice is dedicated to elder law?
- Does she/he concentrate on certain laws?
- Is there a consultation fee, and what is it?
- What information should you bring to the first meeting?

NAELA is not a free referral service for attorneys; however, if you send them a stamped, self-addressed envelope they will mail you a brochure on how to choose the right attorney for you. For $25 they will send you a copy of their Experience Registry of more than 350 elder law attorneys in the United States, with their legal specialties.

PHONE: 520-881-4005

NAELA has attorneys in the Texas cities listed below. Their Experience Registry will provide additional information about these attorneys.

Amarillo	Austin	Baytown
Beaumont	Bellaire	Brenham
Bryan	Corpus Christi	Dallas
Desoto	Edinburg	El Paso
Euless	Fort Worth	Gainesville
Houston	Humble	Hurst
Katy	Longview	Lubbock
McAllen	Midland	Nacogdoches
Refugio	Richmond	San Angelo
San Antonio	The Woodlands	Tyler
Victoria		

The following section lists several attorneys who specialize in elder law. While located in central Texas, they would be willing to handle cases across the state or possibly recommend an attorney in your area.

D. ELLIOT BRANSON, LLP

Elliot Branson works in the Law Offices of Preston Henrichson, P.C., and he is a member of the National Academy of Elder Law Attorneys, Inc. (NAELA). He specializes in helping elderly and retired citizens find the best way to preserve their wealth and their estates, and also to receive the full benefits of Social Security, Medicare, retirement, and other resources to which they are entitled. Initial visits are free. He offers 25% off will preparations when you mention you were referred to him by this book.

ADDRESS:	222 W. Cano St.
	Edinburg
PHONE:	210-383-3535

DAVID R. FREEMAN, LLP

Experienced in many facets of the law, David Freeman has a special interest in contract law, real estate law, will preparation, probate, and trusts.

AGE:	50
DISCOUNT:	25% off will preparation when you
	mention this book
ADDRESS:	100 Congress Ave., Suite 2000
	Austin
PHONE:	512-469-3780

PATRICK E. LACY, LLP

Mr. Lacy primarily practices elder law work in the Euless area and is a member of the National Academy of Elder Law Attorneys, Inc. (NAELA).

PHONE:	817-267-9580

WILLIAM S. NEWBERRY, JR., LLP

Mr. Newberry will be happy to meet with you to discuss your legal needs, and will not charge seniors 50 and better for the initial visit.

AGE: 50
DISCOUNT: Free initial visit
ADDRESS: 11782 Jolleyville Rd.
              Austin
PHONE: 512-219-4098

G. GAYE THOMPSON, LLP AND
A. LYNN TIEMANN, LLP

The firm of Thompson & Tiemann LLP does work primarily in the field of elder law. They're particularly interested in serving the senior population (both attorneys are over 50). They specialize in wills, probate, guardianship, estate planning, and other facets of elder law.

AGE: Unspecified
DISCOUNT: One-half off their hourly rate of $150 for
              the first hour's consultation when you men-
              tion this book
ADDRESS: 1206 S. Congress Ave.
              Austin
PHONE: 512-444-6171

TAXES

IRS SALE OF PRINCIPAL HOME*

Be sure to consult IRS Tax Publication #554 *Tax Information for Older Americans* (and your tax consultant) when you consider selling your principal residence. Please refer to Tax

* (Source: Publication #554, Cat. No. 15102R, *1995 Tax Information for Older Americans,* Department of the Treasury, Internal Revenue Service)

Questions & Help at the end of this chapter for the phone number to call to have Publication #554 mailed to your home. This tax law for the sale of your principal home is a once-in-a-lifetime good deal for older American homeowners.

You can save money on your taxes if you meet the IRS age, ownership, and use tests. If you're married on the date of the sale and file a separate return, you can choose to exclude $62,500 of the gain on your sale, or $125,000 if you're filing a joint return.

Age, Ownership, and Use Tests:

1. You were 55 or older on the date of the sale.
2. During the five-year period ending on the date of the sale you:
   - Owned your main home for at least three years, and
   - Lived in your main home for at least three years.
3. Neither you nor your spouse have ever excluded gain on the sale of a home after July 26, 1978.

IRS STANDARD DEDUCTION AT 65

Don't forget to let the IRS know you've turned 65 (or if you are blind) when you do your next tax return, because you'll see a hefty increase in your standard deduction. You'll find this information on a chart called "Standard Deduction Chart for People Age 65 or Older or Blind."

STATE PROPERTY TAX EXEMPTION*

You may be eligible for home exemptions on your Texas property taxes. Call the Texas State Comptroller's Office—Property Tax Division in Austin at 800-252-9121 to request a copy of the *Texas Property Taxes* brochure. Remember that claiming the homestead

---

* (Source: *1996 Texas Property Taxes,* Comptroller of Public Accounts, Tax Publications)

exemption on your residence is free. In the past, scam artists have been trying to "sell" this to unsuspecting Texans.

Age 65 or Older Homeowners

- If you are 65 or older on January 1, your residence home-stead will qualify for a $10,000 homestead exemption for the school taxes on your home's value, in addition to the $5,000 (homestead) exemption for all Texas homeowners. In addition to the $10,000 exemption for school taxes, any taxing unit—including a school district—can offer an additional exemption of at least $3,000 for taxpayers age 65 or older.

- Once you receive an over-65 homestead exemption, you get a tax ceiling for that home on your total school taxes. The school taxes on your home cannot increase as long as you own and live in that home. The tax ceiling is the amount you pay in the year that you qualify for the over-65 home-owner exemption. The school taxes on your home may go below the ceiling, but the school taxes will not be more than the amount of your ceiling. However, your tax ceiling can go up if you improve your home, such as adding a garage or game room to your home.

- Homeowners age 65 or older who apply for the exemptions may also pay their home taxes in installments.

The *Texas Property Taxes* brochure also lists Texas property tax exemptions for Texas residents who are either (1) a veteran who was disabled while serving with the U.S. armed forces, or (2) the surviving spouse or child (under 18 years of age and unmarried) of a disabled veteran or of a member of the armed forces who was killed while on active duty.

Tax Questions and Help

If you have tax questions or would like help doing your taxes, there are several places to check. The IRS has a program called Tax Counseling for the Elderly for those 60 and over:

Dallas:	214-742-2440
Houston:	713-541-0440
Texas:	800-829-1040 (if Dallas or Houston isn't a local call)

To help you understand your current tax situation better, call the IRS forms hotline at 800-829-3676 (800 TAX FORM), and they'll mail you these free publications:

- Pub. #524—*Credit for the Elderly or Disabled*
- Pub. #554—*Tax Information for Older Americans*
- Pub. #575—*Pension and Annuity Income*
- Pub. #721—*IRS Tax Help*

There's a watchdog group in Washington looking out for the rights of older Americans. Write to them for a copy of their free publication *Protecting Older Americans Against Overpayment of Income Taxes.* Write or call them and let them hear your concerns.*

Special Committee on Aging
U.S. Senate
Washington, D.C. 20410
202-224-5364

AARP. You can also call your local AARP chapter if you're a member or join for $8 a year. Many of them offer a program for tax help. Refer to Senior Organizations for phone numbers.

---

* (Source: Lesko, M. with Martello, M.A., *Free Stuff for Seniors,* Kensington: Information USA, Inc., 1995, pp. 290–293.)

Area Agencies on Aging. Many of the Texas Area Agencies on Aging, funded by the Federal Department on Aging, provide free tax assistance for seniors. Refer to Chapter 13, Senior Organizations, for a list of Texas locations and their phone numbers.

Medical and Dental Services

HEARING SERVICES

GEORGETOWN HEARING AID CENTER

Call Jim Cearnal for a free in-home hearing test in the Georgetown area. Georgetown Hearing Aid Center has been providing quality service in Williamson County for eight years. They offer senior discounts on sales and service. They also do repairs on hearing aid products.

AGE: 55
DISCOUNT: 10%
PHONE: Georgetown
            800-856-4691

HOSPITALS

AUSTIN DIAGNOSTIC CLINIC (ADC) CLASSICS CLUB

ADC is a network of over 145 physicians practicing in 24 medical specialties at 20 locations throughout the Austin and San Marcos area. Membership in ADC's Classics Club is free for seniors 55 years of age. Your membership entitles you to a wide range of services and discounts, including:

- Health and wellness classes
- Seminars and workshops on topics such as self-defense, healthy cooking, and computer basics
- *Classics Club Quarterly* newsletter
- Discount prescription card for a network of 40,000 pharmacies
- Discounts on medical equipment, travel, prescription footwear, health clubs, restaurants, and more
- Discounted or free health screenings and flu shots
- Day tours to many Texas destinations each month

AGE: 55
PHONE: 512-703-6765

BAYLOR HEALTH CARE SYSTEM 55PLUS

55PLUS is a senior membership program that Baylor developed in 1987 to help meet the special needs of the growing population of seniors in the Dallas/Fort Worth metroplex. With over 139,000 members, Baylor 55PLUS is among the largest of all hospital-based senior membership programs.

AGE: 55
PHONE: 800-4BAYLOR (800-422-9567)
INTERNET: http://www.bhcs.com

This program provides the following benefits for members when they're well or ill.

Benefits when you're ill include:

- Physician referral service at 800-4BAYLOR
- Complimentary transportation to and from the hospital when you live within a 25-mile radius of a Baylor Medical Center
- Advance registration three days prior to your admission to prevent lengthy waits the day of admission
- Guest representative and concierge desk available for you and your family during your stay

- Complimentary guest meal coupon for a friend or family member for each day of your stay
- Two complimentary parking tokens for your visitors for each day of your hospital stay
- Complimentary television and telephone in your room at no additional charge (long-distance charges are extra)
- Complimentary homemaker service in your home for up to six hours of light housekeeping, meal preparation, and grocery shopping when your doctor approves your request for this service

Benefits when you're well include:

- Baylor 55PLUS's award-winning magazine *The Advisor*
- Health screenings, classes, and seminars throughout the year
- 55PLUS credit card
- Baylor Health Care System Credit Union membership
- Discount dining card
- Pharmacy Plus benefit package

The Baylor Health Care System encompasses the following facilities:

Baylor Garland Family Practice Center • 972-495-4955

Baylor Family Health Center, Colleyville Family Medicine 817-498-9920

Baylor Family Health Center, Flower Mound Family Medicine • 972-724-1707

Baylor Family Health Center at Mesquite • 972-682-4100

Baylor Family Health Center, Southlake Family Medicine 817-424-3366

Baylor Family Health Center, Family Medical Center at North Garland • 972-495-5888

Baylor Pediatric Center • 214-823-2525

Dallas Diagnostic Association of Garland • 972-494-6235

Dallas Diagnostic Association • 972-991-6000

Dallas Diagnostic Association of Richardson • 972-498-8650

Ellis County Diagnostic Clinic, Midlothian • 972-723-1474

Ellis County Diagnostic Clinic, Waxahachie • 972-923-1686

Esters Family Medical Clinic • 972-790-5209

Family Medical Center at Garland • 972-272-6561

Family Medical Center at Rockwall • 972-771-9155

North Texas Health Care Associates • 972-869-4664

Richardson Health Center • 972-498-4990

Ennis Community Health Center • 972-875-0988

Waxahachie Community Health Center • 972-923-7346

COLUMBIA HEALTH CARE

Columbia has a network of hospitals across the country. When you dial their toll-free number, you'll be connected to the Columbia Hospital nearest you. Some of these hospitals have individual senior membership programs, and many of them honor the Senior Friends membership card (eligible at age 50). Please refer to Chapter 13, Senior Organizations, for more information about Senior Friends.

AGE: 50
PHONE: 800-COLUMBIA (800-348-4886)

Daughters of Charity Corporation Facilities*

The following medical facilities are owned by the Daughters of Charity who offer many senior benefits through their Seton Good Health Club program. You'll need to call the facility near you for more details on their specific program and enrollment, but their benefits are offered to anyone 65 or better. Membership is free, and your card is nontransferrable. You'll need to carry your card with you at all times to access the services.

AGE: 65
COST: Free membership

As a member, your benefits will include:

- 50% discount on parking in the parking garage, where available
- Discounts on medical equipment
- Discounts in the cafeterias and gift shops
- Free television and telephone in your hospital room (long-distance charges are extra)
- Free transportation for those in need for same-day surgery or overnight hospital stay (15 mile radius)
- Free subscription to *Good Health* magazine
- Physician Referral Line
- Low-cost classes, seminars, and clinics designed especially for seniors
- Rental pagers available for a small monthly fee

* (Source: *Join the Club!*, Providence Good Health Club)

Austin

Brackenridge Hospital
601 E. 15th St.
512-476-6461

Children's Hospital
601 E. 15th St.
512-480-1818

Seton Medical Center
1201 W. 38th St.
512-323-1000

Seton Northwest Hospital
11113 Research Blvd.
512-795-1000

Waco

Providence Health Center
6701 Medical Pkwy.
817-751-4000

Membership in Providence Health Center's Good Health Club starts at age 55; members are encouraged to use the six-tenths-of-a-mile fitness track that encircles the Health Center campus, and a discount at the Waco Family Y is extended to members.

MEMORIAL HERMANN HEALTHCARE SYSTEM 55+

The Memorial Hermann Healthcare System hospitals are located throughout the greater Houston area. The free Memorial 55+ membership program offers the following 11 reasons to join:

- 20% cafeteria discount at any of their hospitals
- Free dining card offering 20% discounts at 350 Texas restaurants

- Attractively priced travel announced quarterly for members and their guests
- Round-the-clock health information by calling 222-CARE and selecting a health topic
- Private room upgrade (subject to availability at the time of hospitalization)
- Free Rx Memorial 55+ Discount Prescription Card program offering savings from 10% to over 50% through a national network of 40,000 chain and independent pharmacies
- Health and wellness classes
- Physician referral service
- Subscription to Memorial's publications

AGE: 55
PHONE: 713-222-CARE

The following facilities are part of the Memorial Healthcare System:

Bellville Community Hospital • 409-865-3165

Columbus Community Hospital • 409-732-9242

Memorial Hospital–Memorial City • 713-932-3000

Memorial Hospital Northwest • 713-867-2000

Memorial Hospital Pasadena • 713-477-0411

Memorial Hospital Southeast • 281-929-6100

Memorial Hospital Southwest • 713-776-5000

Memorial Hospital–The Woodlands • 281-364-2300

Rice Medical Center Hospital • 409-234-5571

METHODIST HEALTH CARE SYSTEM PRIORITYONE

Methodist Hospital in Houston offers seniors 50 and better their PriorityOne program. Your annual membership fee entitles you to discounts, benefits, and services that include:

- Methodist's speaker's bureau
- Audio health library
- Physician referral and health information service
- Free subscriptions to *Journal,* Methodist's award-winning magazine, and the PriorityOne quarterly newsletter
- Discounts of 10% to 70% on everything from prescriptions to travel
- Membership in the OASIS (Older Adult Service and Information System) program for educational, social, and travel opportunities
- Methodist's services and privileges, including private room upgrade (when available) for no additional charge, discounted parking, and a discount at the Methodist Health Care System's Tower Cafe

AGE:	50
COST:	$12 for singles, $20 for couples
ADDRESS:	Methodist Health Care System
	6565 Fannin
	Houston
PHONE:	713-793-1432
INTERNET:	http://www.methodisthealth.com

ST. DAVID'S MEDICAL CENTER AND SOUTH AUSTIN MEDICAL CENTER

St. David's and South Austin medical centers are Columbia Hospitals that offer senior discounts and honor Senior Friends members. If you're 50 years old or better, you can park for free at both hospitals and enjoy a discount at their cafeterias whether you're a patient or just visiting one. You may be asked to show your driver's license.

AGE: 50
DISCOUNT: 20% at the cafeteria and free parking
ADDRESS: St. David's Medical Center
              12221 MoPac Expwy. North
              Austin
              512-901-1000

              South Austin Medical Center
              919 E. 32nd St.
              Austin
              512-476-7111

ST. ELIZABETH HOSPITAL HEALTH PARTNERS

St. Elizabeth Hospital offers the Health Partners program to adults over 50 years of age as a community service to Beaumont and Southeast Texas. To become a member, call and request an application be mailed to you.

AGE: 50
PHONE: 409-899-CARE (in Beaumont)
              800-323-4713 (outside Beaumont
              calling area)

Members of Health Partners receive the following benefits:

- Health screenings for blood sugar, blood pressure, and cholesterol
- Educational programs
- Discounts from participating area merchants
- Interest-free hospital payment plans
- *Health* newsletter
- Private hospital room at semi-private rates (subject to availability. Discounted rates do not apply to special care units)

- Membership to Aging Resource Library at Parkdale Mall
- Pre-registration for hospital admission
- Health advisor as your senior advisor to help with your health-care needs

ST. MARY HOSPITAL PRIME TIME CLUB

Port Arthur seniors 50 and better can participate in the Prime Time Club for free! This community service program offers members:

- Educational programs
- *Prime Time News* monthly newsletter
- St. Mary discounts including private room at semi-private room rates (subject to availability at admission), discounts on meals in the Harbor Room, and discounts on hospital bills
- Customized exercise program at the Wellness Center and access to walking track in the Fitness Center
- Health screenings throughout the year announced in the newsletter
- Savings available from area merchants
- Reserved parking for members only
- Complimentary meals for member's spouse when member is an inpatient

AGE: 50
ADDRESS: St. Mary Hospital
              3600 Gates Blvd.
              Port Arthur
PHONE: 409-983-1602

SISTERS OF CHARITY HEALTH CARE SYSTEM VIP ADVANTAGE

For a one-time $5 application fee, seniors 55 and better can become lifetime members of the VIP Advantage Program at these two Sisters of Charity Health Care Hospitals. Membership entitles you to:

- Extras during a hospital stay, including discounted parking, discounts at hospital gift shop and cafeteria, and room upgrades, subject to availability
- Special rates on goods and services from participating merchants
- Newsletter every three months
- Invitations to seminars
- Classes and health screenings

ADDRESSES: St. Joseph Hospital
              1919 LaBranch
              Houston
              713-757-7552

              St. John Hospital
              18100 Hospital Blvd.
              Nassau Bay
              972-333-5503

PHARMACIES

ACE DRUG MART

There are five Ace Drug Marts in the Hill Country, and they're owned by two different individuals. While all of the Ace Drug Marts listed here offer seniors a discount, there are differences between the two sets of stores.

These benefits are offered at the following two Ace Drug Marts:

AGE: 55
DISCOUNT: 10% off all prescriptions
              Free delivery to zip codes: 78745,
              78704, 78743, 78702, 78703, 78746

ADDRESSES: Austin
611 W. Ben White Blvd.
512-444-2391

Elgin
Located in the Super S Store
214 US Hwy. 290
512-281-3465

These Ace Drug Marts carry prescription drugs and a full range of medical equipment including ostomy supplies. They also deliver medical equipment to Travis County and the four surrounding counties. Owner Jim Kotrla said, "If we don't have it, we can get it." They will prepare unit dose packaging and other special packaging upon request. These Ace Drug Marts will take assignments, bill Medicare, and bill insurance companies for you.

The following three Ace Drug Marts in Austin offer these benefits to senior customers:

AGE: 55
DISCOUNT: 10% off everything, except magazines and tobacco products
ADDRESSES: 1508 W. 35th St.
512-454-2653

6305 Cameron Rd.
512-454-2541

5304 Burnet Rd.
512-452-0185

B&B PHARMACY*

Visit B&B Pharmacy when you're in the Pampa area. Pharmacist and owner Dennis (Denny) Roark promises to provide you with friendly, fast, and dependable service.

* (Source: Internet - http://www.pan-tex.net/usr/b/bbpharm/)

AGE: 60
DISCOUNT: 10% off prescriptions only
ADDRESS: 300 N. Ballard
                Pampa
PHONE: 806-665-5778
                800-273-0927
                806-665-2892 (Emergency)
FAX: 806-669-7592

Other benefits to customers include:

- First Care HMO approved
- Free delivery
- Fast service

DRUG EMPORIUM

At your local Drug Emporium, you'll find prescription and over-the-counter drugs, greeting cards, a nice wine selection, cosmetics, snacks, and a large variety of items for the home.

Some Drug Emporiums offer a two-day senior appreciation discount promotion approximately once a month. They'll advertise this promotion in local newspapers and offer seniors a 10% discount on everything in the store except prescriptions, alcohol, and cigarettes. Call your local Drug Emporium for details on their senior discounts.

AGE: 55
DISCOUNT: 10% on advertised days

RANDALLS PHARMACY

The pharmacy in your "remarkable" Randalls grocery store offers a Senior Coupon card. After you fill five prescriptions, they'll give seniors $5 off the next prescription filled.

AGE: 60
DISCOUNT: $5 off after five prescriptions filled

VISION SERVICES

GENE RODGERS OPTICAL

Gene Rodgers Optical in Austin has been a family-owned and operated business since 1954, and they offer seniors 55 and better a discount on glasses.

AGE:	55
DISCOUNT:	15% off glasses
ADDRESS:	2700 W. Anderson Ln.
	Austin
PHONE:	512-451-7316

Mr. Rodgers is a certified and registered optician—a license that is not yet required by the state of Texas and that you may not find at your discount frame shop. He attends continuing education to keep his certification, and can fill all prescriptions.

TEXAS STATE OPTICAL (TSO)

Ms. Ann Deen at TSO corporate headquarters polled their TSO offices and provided the following detailed information regarding senior discounts. NOTE: Discounts are not good with any other discounts, coupons, or Medicaid.

Alice

Gary Cloud, O.D.
559 Hwy. 281 North
512-664-1021

Discount Age:	65
Discount Percentage:	20%
Discount on Exam:	N
Discount on Materials:	Y

Amarillo

William R. Chafin, O.D.
2110 S. Western St.
806-355-9711

Discount Age:	65
Discount Percentage:	15%
Discount on Exam:	Y
Discount on Materials:	Y

Austin

Terence E. Jansen, O.D.
133 W. Oltorf St.
512-442-2308
Discount Age:	60
Discount Percentage:	15%
Discount on Exam:	Y
Discount on Materials:	Y

Terence E. Jansen, O.D.
6801 I-35 South
512-441-8924
Discount Age:	60
Discount Percentage:	15%
Discount on Exam:	Y
Discount on Materials:	Y

Doug Clark, O.D.
5501-B IH-35 North
512-451-0229
Discount Age:	60 +
Discount Percentage:	10%
Discount on Exam:	N
Discount on Materials:	Y

Doug Clark, O.D.
2900 W. Anderson Ln.
512-451-2072
Discount Age:	60 +
Discount Percentage:	10%
Discount on Exam:	N
Discount on Materials:	Y

Gregg Kamentz, O.D.
2901 Capitol of Texas Hwy.
512-327-3605
Discount Age:	65
Discount Percentage:	15%
Discount on Exam:	N
Discount on Materials:	Y

Bay City

Earl Brown, O.D.
3612 Ave. F
409-244-1440
Discount Age:	60
Discount Percentage:	20%
Discount on Exam:	Y
Discount on Materials:	Y

Baytown

Richard Hutto, O.D.
6956 Garth Rd.
281-421-1243
Discount Age:	62
Discount Percentage:	15%
Discount on Exam:	N
Discount on Materials:	Y

B. Warford, O.D., Richard
   Hutto, O.D.
301 W. Texas
281-427-7374
Discount Age:	62
Discount Percentage:	15%
Discount on Exam:	N
Discount on Materials:	Y

Beaumont

Don Reeves, O.D.
138 Gateway
409-835-4509
Discount Age:	65
Discount Percentage:	10%
Discount on Exam:	N
Discount on Materials:	Y

Brian Blount, O.D.
302 Parkdale Mall
409-892-3677
Discount Age: 55
Discount Percentage: 10%
Discount on Exam: N
Discount on Materials: Y

Brenham

Donald Rexroad, O.D.
801-B S. Market St.
409-836-1166
Discount Age: 65
Discount Percentage: 10%
Discount on Exam: N
Discount on Materials: Y

Bryan

G. D. Phillips, O.D.
3030 E. 29th St.
409-731-8446
Discount Age: 55
Discount Percentage: 10%
Discount on Exam: N
Discount on Materials: Y

Cleburne

Robert Gracey, O.D.
1607 W. Henderson North
817-645-7733
Discount Age: 62
Discount Percentage: 15%
Discount on Exam: N
Discount on Materials: Y

College Station

R. J. Maggs, O.D.
2414-A Texas Ave. South
409-764-0010
Discount Age: 55
Discount Percentage: 10%
Discount on Exam: N
Discount on Materials: Y

Conroe

Michael Nell, O.D.
1148 W. Dallas
409-756-8622
Discount Age: 65
Discount Percentage: 10%
Discount on Exam: N
Discount on Materials: Y

Dallas

TSO Red Bird
3027 W. Camp Wisdom Rd.
972-296-1825
Discount Age: 55
  Materials: 55
  Exam: 60
Discount on Exam: 10%
Discount on Materials: 15%

J. O. Rogers, O.D.
2223-B S. Buckner
214-388-4761
Discount Age: 60
Discount Percentage: 20%
Discount on Exam: Y
Discount on Materials: Y

El Paso

Douglas R. Eley, O.D.
9350-B Dyer
915-751-7769

Discount Age:	60
Discount Percentage:	10%
Discount on Exam:	Y
Discount on Materials:	Y

Fort Worth

Benny Askins, O.D.
6212-A Camp Bowie Blvd.
817-737-7294

Discount Age:	55
Discount Percentage:	10%
Discount on Exam:	N
Discount on Materials:	Y

Fredericksburg

Jules W. Dupuy, O.D.
1021 Hwy. 16 South
210-997-2504

Discount Age:	62
Discount Percentage:	10%
Discount on Exam:	N
Discount on Materials:	Y

Gainesville

Clyde McCain, O.D.
311-B E. California
817-668-7254

Discount Age:	65
Discount Percentage: 10% on purchases over $125	
Discount on Exam:	N
Discount on Materials:	Y

Galveston

Kevin Katz, O.D.
515 22nd St.
409-762-8679

Discount Age:	65
Discount Percentage:	15%
Discount on Exam:	Y
Discount on Materials:	Y

Grand Prairie

TSO Grand Prairie
104 W. Main
972-262-4391

Discount Age:	55
Discount Percentage:	15%
Discount on Exam:	Y
Discount on Materials:	Y

Houston

Al Gurin, O.D.
8205 Long Point Rd.
713-468-1113

Discount Age:	60
Discount Percentage:	15%
Discount on Exam:	N
Discount on Materials:	Y

Wayne Maltz, O.D.
5307-B FM 1960 West
281-440-5887

Discount Age:	65
Discount Percentage:	20%
Discount on Exam:	Y
Discount on Materials:	Y

Michael Siegel, O.D.
564 Northwest Mall
713-681-7110
Discount Age: 60
Discount Percentage: 15%
Discount on Exam: N
Discount on Materials: Y

T. Drummond, O.D.
6636-B Harrisburg Blvd.
409-923-7115
Discount Age: 65
Discount Percentage: 10%
Discount on Exam: N
Discount on Materials: Y

TSO Fondren
11127-A Fondren Rd.
713-270-4200
Discount Age: 55
Discount Percentage: 15%
Discount on Exam: Y
Discount on Materials: Y

Angela Marcaccio, O.D.
306 Northline Mall
713-697-2081
Discount Age: 55
Discount on Exam: $10
Discount on Materials: 20%

Richard Redfield, O.D.
12122 Gulf Fwy.
713-944-3826
Discount Age: 60
Discount Percentage: 40%
Discount on Exam: N
Discount on Materials: Y

Linda Matocha, O.D.
603 Memorial City Mall
713-468-7631
Discount Age: 55
Discount on Exam: $10
Discount on Materials: 20%

Stuart Belfer, O.D.
14032-B Memorial at Kirkwood
281-496-1635
Discount Age: 55
Discount Percentage: 15%
Discount on Exam: Y
Discount on Materials: Y

Michael Reade, O.D.
1250 Uvalde Rd.
713-453-2972
Discount Age: 55
Discount on Exam: $10
Discount on Materials: 20%

Michael Reade, O.D.
Brett Donaldson, O.D.
908 Walker St.
713-654-0042
Discount Age: 55
Discount on Exam: $10
Discount on Materials: 20%

Lee Ann Hoven, O.D., Lee N.
   Vu, O.D.
17776 Tomball Pkwy.
281-890-8480
Discount Age: 55
Discount on Exam: $10
Discount on Materials: 20%

Michael Reade, O.D.
Amanda Deleon, O.D.
4850 S. Main
713-523-5109

Discount Age:	55
Discount on Exam:	$10
Discount on Materials:	20%

TSO Inwood
6818 Antoine Dr.
713-956-7292

Discount Age:	55
Discount Percentage:	15%
Discount on Exam:	Y
Discount on Materials:	Y

Aurea Rivera, O.D.
1011 N. Shepherd
713-862-3149

Discount Age:	62
Discount Percentage:	10%
Discount on Exam:	N
Discount on Materials:	Y

Roland G. Montemayor, O.D.
2693 Hwy. 6 South
281-493-1166

Discount Age:	59
Discount Percentage:	15%
Discount on Exam:	N
Discount on Materials:	Y

Marc Gold, O.D.
6328 Telephone Rd.
713-644-2375

Discount Age:	65
Discount Percentage:	15%
Discount on Exam:	N
Discount on Materials:	Y

David Lopez, O.D.
N.J. Oliver, O.D.
724 Meyerland Plaza
713-666-2277

Discount Age:	62
Discount Percentage:	15%
Discount on Exam:	N
Discount on Materials:	Y

Perry Soli, O.D.
8478 Hwy. 6 North
281-550-3600

Discount Age:	60
Discount Percentage:	15%
Discount on Exam:	N
Discount on Materials:	Y

Warren Wacher, O.D.
10001 Westheimer
713-977-0725

Discount Age:	55
Discount Percentage:	15%
Discount on Exam:	Y
Discount on Materials:	Y

George Lipshy, O.D.
379-B Westwood Mall
713-772-4225

Discount Age:	60
Discount Percentage:	15%
Discount on Exam:	Y
Discount on Materials:	Y

Bruce Hoff, O.D.
701 Sharpstown Center
713-981-6021

Discount Age:	60
Discount Percentage:	15%
Discount on Exam:	N
Discount on Materials:	Y

Lee Ann Hoven, O.D.
121 Greenspoint Mall
281-875-6800
Discount Age: 55
Discount on Exam: $10
Discount on Materials: 20%

Samuel Gold, O.D.
711-B Shotwell
713-673-6355
Discount Age: 65
Discount Percentage: 15%
Discount on Exam: N
Discount on Materials: Y

Humble

Simon Yeung, O.D.
19623 Eastex Fwy.
281-446-0103
Discount Age: 55
Discount Percentage: 20%
Discount on Exam: N
Discount on Materials: Y

Kerrville

Jules W. Dupuy, O.D.
205-B W. Water St.
210-896-4044
Discount Age: 62
Discount Percentage: 10%
Discount on Exam: N
Discount on Materials: Y

Kingsville

Gary Cloud, O.D.
2324 S. Brahma Blvd
512-595-5625
Discount Age: 65
Discount Percentage: 20%
Discount on Exam: N
Discount on Materials: Y

Lake Jackson

Sam Shandley, O.D.
120 Hwy. 332 West
409-297-3095
Discount Age: 62
Discount Percentage: 10%
Discount on Exam: N
Discount on Materials: Y

Laredo

Mario Barrera, O.D.
616 W. Calton, Ste. 2
210-722-2022
Discount Age: 60
Discount Percentage on
purchases over $150:   10%
Discount on Exam: N
Discount on Materials: Y

Lewisville

Jeff Harrell, O.D.
1124 W. Main St.
972-221-2561
Discount Age: 65
Discount Percentage: 15%
Discount on Exam: N
Discount on Materials: Y

Liberty

Allen R. Griffin, O.D.
2720 N. Main St.
409-336-5783
Discount Age: 65
Discount Percentage: 15%
Discount on Exam: N
Discount on Materials: Y

Longview

Jeffrey Jones, O.D.
2500 Judson Rd., Ste. B
903-758-5774
Discount Age: 65
Discount Percentage: 10%
Discount on Exam: Y
Discount on Materials: Y

McKinney

Anne K. Webb, O.D.
312 Hwy. 75
972-542-2681
Discount Age: 55
Discount Percentage: 10%
Discount on Exam: Y
Discount on Materials: Y

Nacogdoches

Alva Clevenger, O.D.
4729 N.E. Stalling Dr.
409-564-2634
Discount Age: 62
Discount on Exam: 10%
Discount on Materials: 15%

Nederland

Roger Young, O.D.
1031 Nederland
409-722-6141
Discount Age: 65
Discount Percentage: 10%
Discount on Exam: N
Discount on Materials: Y

New Braunfels

Richard Brodtman, O.D.
101 I-35 West
210-629-1248
Discount Age: 60
Discount Percentage: 15%
Discount on Exam: N
Discount on Materials: 15%

Odessa

Stanley E. Lassa, O.D.
420 N. Grant
915-332-0717
Discount Age: 62
Discount Percentage: 15%
Discount on Exam: N
Discount on Materials: Y

Orange

John Crawford, O.D.
3729 N. 16th St.
409-883-4821
Discount Age: 62
Discount on Exam: 10%
Discount on Materials: 15%

Pasadena

TSO Southmore
407 Pasadena Town Square
713-473-2895
Discount Age:	55
Discount Percentage:	15%
Discount on Exam:	Y
Discount on Materials:	Y

James Mikkelson, O.D.
3610 Spencer Hwy.
713-946-9300
Discount Age:	55
Discount on Exam:	$10
Discount on Materials:	20%

Family Eye Associates
James Mikkelson, O.D.
825 E. Southmore
713-473-2020
Discount Age:	55
Discount on Exam:	$10
Discount on Materials:	20%

Port Arthur

Barry Davis, O.D.
3429-B Twin City Hwy.
409-962-5796
Discount Age:	65
Discount Percentage:	10%
Discount on Exam:	N
Discount on Materials:	Y

Richardson

William Ponder, O.D.
49 Richardson Heights
972-235-7101
Discount Age:	55
Discount Percentage:	15%
Discount on Exam:	Y
Discount on Materials:	Y

Rosenberg

Leroy E. Knekow, O.D.
5172-B Ave. H
281-342-3554
Discount Age:	65
Discount Percentage:	15%
Discount on Exam:	Y
Discount on Materials:	Y

Round Rock

James R. Rogers, O.D.
1202 N. I-35
512-255-7846
Discount Age:	60
Discount Percentage:	15%
Discount on Exam:	N
Discount on Materials:	Y

San Angelo

Bryan McDaniel, O.D.
113-B S. Chadbourne
915-653-6897
Discount Age:	60
Discount Percentage:	15%
Discount on Exam:	N
Discount on Materials:	Y

San Antonio

TSO McCreless
1000 McCreless Mall
210-533-3316
Discount Age:	55
Discount Percentage:	15%
Discount on Exam on Mondays:	10%
Discount on Materials:	Y

Gerardo R. Noriega, O.D.
16111 San Pedro
210-545-5755
Discount Age: 55
Discount Percentage: 25%
Discount on Exam: Y
Discount on Materials: Y

San Marcos

Stephen Stanfield, O.D.
215 Springtown Center
512-353-8932
Discount Age: 60
Discount Percentage: 25%
Discount on Exam: Y
Discount on Materials: Y

Silsbee

John T. Queen, O.D.
125 N. 5th St.
409-385-5262
Discount Age: 55
Discount Percentage: 15%
Discount on Exam: N
Discount on Materials: Y

Spring

L. J. Perdue, O.D.
18555 Kuykendahl Rd.
281-370-9083
Discount Age: 62
Discount Percentage: 10%
Discount on Exam: N
Discount on Materials: Y

Stephenville

Monty Banks, O.D.
101 N. Dole
817-968-4133
Discount Age: 62
Discount Percentage: 10%
Discount on Exam: N
Discount on Materials: Y

Texarkana

TSO Towne West
2315 Richmond Rd.
903-838-0783
Discount Age: 55
Discount Percentage: 15%
Discount on Exam: Y
Discount on Materials: Y

Tyler

Clyde Houston, O.D.
4524 S. Broadway
903-581-1530
Discount Age: 65
Discount Percentage on
purchases over $150:   10%
Discount on Exam: N
Discount on Materials: Y

Vernon

C. Chrietzberg, O.D.
701 E. US Hwy. 287
817-552-7791
Discount Age:
Women   63
Men   65
Discount Percentage: 15%
Discount on Exam: N
Discount on Materials: Y

Wichita Falls

J. B. Temple, O.D.		Jerry Young, O.D.	
908-B Indiana Ave.		462-A Sikes Center	
817-766-3209		817-691-0200	
Discount Age:		Discount Age:	
Women	63	Women	63
Men	65	Men	65
Discount Percentage:	15%	Discount Percentage:	15%
Discount on Exam:	N	Discount on Exam:	N
Discount on Materials:	Y	Discount on Materials:	Y

DENTAL SERVICES

PATRICK E. DANIELS, D.M.D.

A prosthodontist, Dr. Daniels specializes in removable appliances, dentures, and partials in the Austin area. Call his office to schedule an appointment for Mondays, Tuesdays, or Fridays.

AGE:	60
DISCOUNT:	10% off final bill
ADDRESS:	1500 W. 38th St., Ste. 56
	Austin
PHONE:	512-458-8497

DONALD H. NAEVE, D.D.S. & ASSOCIATES
MELINDA S. JONES, D.D.S.

Family dentistry for adults and children with a television video-recorder running your favorite movie over each dental chair is available from these Austin area dentists.

AGE:	65
DISCOUNT:	10% off final bill
ADDRESS:	4000 Manchaca Rd.
	Austin
PHONE:	512-441-2098

This practice has been serving Austin since 1974. New patients and emergencies are welcome, and they offer the following services:

- Teeth bleaching
- Cosmetic dentistry (bonding and sealants)
- Nitrous oxide sedation upon request
- Insurance processed

ROBERT G. WILLIAMS, D.D.S., ABFO, INC.

Located in the Preston Forest Shopping Center approximately one mile south of I-635 in Dallas, Dr. Williams provides dental care with a discount.

AGE:	60
DISCOUNT:	10% off all services
ADDRESS:	11661 Preston Rd., Ste. 141
	Dallas
PHONE:	214-361-7933

- General dentistry (fillings, extractions, crown and bridge-work, dentures, partials)
- Cosmetic dentistry (whitening, closing spaces without orthodontics, porcelain veneer jackets)
- Diagnostic services (X-rays, fiber optic dental photography)
- Dental appliances (sport mouthguards, anti-snoring appliances, TMJ splints)
- Mild sedation for patients with anxiety
- Periodontal (gum therapy and routine maintenance with a dental hygienist)

They will file insurance for you, offer a 12-month, no interest payment plan, and accept MasterCard, VISA, Discover, and American Express.

Movies and the Performing Arts

ACT III (PRESIDIO) THEATRES

Enjoy a movie at any ACT III (Presidio) Theatre anytime at the following price for seniors.

AGE: 55
COST: $3.50 anytime

CINEMARK THEATRES

Enjoy a movie at one of Cinemark's 67 theatres across the state.

AGE: 55
COST: $3.25 anytime

DOBIE THEATRE

The Dobie Theatre, located in Dobie Mall near the University of Texas, shows an eclectic variety of movies and offers a senior discount:

AGE: 65
DISCOUNT: $3.50 anytime
ADDRESS: Dobie Mall

                        2021 Guadalupe St.
                        Austin
PHONE: 512-472-3456

General Cinema

This chain of 34 theaters not only offers an individual senior discount, but it'll lower the price even more if you bring a bunch of your friends! Call ahead and bring a group of 20 seniors, and they'll lower the price to $3.25 per person.

AGE: 65
COST: $3.75 anytime

United Artists Theatres

This movie theater chain operates Austin's only virtual theme park in Lakeline Mall. There are many other United Artists Theatres throughout the state.

AGE: 60
COST: $3.50 anytime

BALLET

Ballet Austin*

The Company was founded and incorporated as the Austin Ballet Society in 1956. Since that time, Ballet Austin has grown from 12 dancers to 24 professional dancers. Lambros Lambrou is the Artistic Director.

AGE: 65
DISCOUNT: 15% off single tickets (not on season tickets)
PHONE: 512-476-2163

Performances are held on the University of Texas campus at the Bass Concert Hall. In addition to evening perfor-

---

* (Source: *The History,* Ballet Austin)

mances, Ballet Austin offers Sunday matinees at 2 p.m. for scheduled performances.

FORT WORTH–DALLAS BALLET

Performances are held in Fort Worth at the Tarrant County Convention Center, 1111 Houston St.

AGE: 65
DISCOUNT: 10% off season tickets
HONORS: AARP (discount at age 50)
PHONE: 817-377-9988

HOUSTON BALLET

Offering performances at the Wortham Center and Jones Hall, the Houston Ballet offers discounted tickets for seniors.

AGE: 65
COST: $10 per ticket
PHONE: 800-828-ARTS

Tickets must be purchased in person at the ticket offices at the Wortham Center, 550 Prairie, or Jones Hall, 615 Louisiana, one hour prior to curtain. A photo identification showing your birth date is required. These tickets are subject to availability.

LIVE THEATER

ALLEY THEATRE

The Alley Theatre in Houston celebrated its 50th anniversary in 1996. Seniors are seated for half-price when they purchase tickets the day of the show either in person or by phone. This senior offer is good for every performance except Friday and Saturday evenings. The Alley Theatre offers performances every day except Monday at 514 Texas Avenue (Texas and Louisiana).

AGE: 65
DISCOUNT: 50%

ESTHER'S FOLLIES

If you're in the mood for irreverent comedy where no public figure is safe, you've got to see Esther's Follies when you're in Austin! They're located on 6th Street and Red River in Austin's entertainment district, and offer seniors a discount unless the show is sold out.

AGE: 55
DISCOUNT: $2
ADDRESS: 525 E. 6th St.
                 Austin
PHONE: 512-320-0553

Performances:

Thursdays: 8 p.m. (senior price $8)
Fridays: 8 p.m. (senior price $10)
Saturdays: 8 p.m. and 10 p.m. (senior price $12)

GALVESTON ISLAND OUTDOOR AMPHITHEATRE*

Enjoy live Broadway musicals under the stars at Galveston Island Outdoor Amphitheatre. There's plenty of free parking located at the entrance to the amphitheatre. Conveniences for individuals needing special assistance include shuttle from the parking lot to the amphitheatre, designated handicap parking, easy wheelchair access, and signed performances for the hearing-impaired (with advance notice).

AGE: 55
DISCOUNT: $2 off (can't use with other discounts)
PHONE: 800-54-SHOWS

---

*(Source: *Live Broadway Musicals on Galveston Island,* Lone Star Performing Arts Association, Inc.)

THE GRAND 1894 OPERA HOUSE

This is the place to enjoy live Broadway musicals in Galveston in a majestic restored 1,008 seat theater. Conveniences for individuals needing special assistance include easy wheelchair access and signed performances for the hearing-impaired (with advance notice).

AGE:	55
DISCOUNT:	$2 off (can't use with other discounts)
PHONE:	800-54-SHOWS

LIVE OAK THEATRE*

Live Oak Theatre at the historic State Theatre on Congress Avenue in Austin celebrated their 15th anniversary in 1996.

AGE:	65
DISCOUNT:	$2 off any performance
PHONE:	512-472-5143

Performances:

Wednesdays–Saturdays:	8 p.m.
Sundays:	6 p.m.

ZACHARY SCOTT THEATRE CENTER**

Spend a magical evening at the Zachary Scott Theatre in Austin.

AGE:	65
DISCOUNT:	$2 off any performance
PHONE:	512-476-0541
INTERNET:	http://www.zachscott.com

---

 * (Source: *Live Oak Theatre at the State*, Live Oak Productions)
** (Source: *Zachary Scott Theatre Center—Magic Happens*, Zachary Scott Theatre Center)

Performances:

Thursdays:	8 p.m. (senior price $13)
Fridays:	8 p.m. (senior price $16)
Saturdays:	8 p.m. (senior price $16)
Sundays:	2:30 p.m. (senior price $13)

Opera

Austin Lyric Opera*

The Austin Lyric Opera celebrated its 10th birthday in 1996. Since that first curtain went up, they have grown into a nationally recognized organization. Enjoy the Austin Lyric Opera at the UT Bass Concert Hall at East Campus and 23rd St. They offer Friday and Saturday performances at 8 p.m., a Sunday performance at 3 p.m., and a Monday performance at 7 p.m.

AGE:	65
DISCOUNT:	$3 (off single tickets, but not off season tickets)
PHONE:	800-31-OPERA

Fort Worth Opera**

The Fort Worth Opera celebrated its 50th anniversary in 1996, making it the oldest opera company in Texas. Performances of the Fort Worth Opera will be at the Tarrant County Convention Center until they move to the Nancy Lee and Perry R. Bass Performance Hall in the 1997–98 season. They offer performances on Friday evening at 7 p.m. and Sunday afternoon at 2 p.m.

AGE:	60
DISCOUNT:	20% off single tickets
	15% off season tickets
PHONE:	817-731-0833

---

* (Source: *Austin Lyric Opera 10th Anniversary Season 1996–97*, Austin Lyric Opera)

** (Source: *Celebrating 50 Years of Excellence*, Fort Worth Opera)

HOUSTON GRAND OPERA

Spend an evening or afternoon with the Houston Grand Opera at the Wortham Center.

AGE:	65
COST:	$21 per ticket (regular price $56 weekday, $66 weekend)
ADDRESS:	550 Prairie
	Houston
PHONE:	800-828-ARTS

Evening Performances. Tickets must be purchased in person beginning at noon on the day of the performance and are subject to availability. Each purchaser must show his or her photo identification with birth date.

Sunday Matinee Performances. Tickets may be purchased by phone or in person beginning at noon on Saturday. The performance box office opens one-half hour before curtain. Tickets are sold in the Orchestra 1A side sections. You must show your photo identification to pick up the tickets. The tickets are subject to availability, and are not guaranteed for all performances.

PERFORMING ARTS

HOUSTON SOCIETY FOR THE PERFORMING ARTS

The Houston Society for the Performing Arts offers performances at Jones Hall and the Wortham Center.

AGE:	65
DISCOUNT:	50%
ADDRESS:	Wortham Center
	550 Prairie
	Jones Hall
	615 Louisiana
PHONE:	800-828-ARTS

Tickets must be purchased, in person, anytime the day of the performance and are subject to availability. Each purchaser must show a photo identification showing his or her birth date (i.e., one ID per person).

Sunday Matinee Performances. Discounted tickets may be purchased by phone or in person beginning on Saturdays. The performance box office opens one hour prior to curtain on Sundays. You must show your photo identification to pick up the tickets. The tickets are subject to availability and may be purchased for any seating section that is available.

SYMPHONY

THE AMARILLO SYMPHONY

The Amarillo Symphony makes a special effort to welcome seniors to performances by offering special seating and pricing for seniors 65 and better. Their regular series of performances are held at the Amarillo Convention Center Auditorium at 3rd and Buchanan. Special senior seating and tickets are $5. Senior tickets and seating for the Randel Chamber Orchestra three-concert series are $5 for each performance. The Harrington String Quartet performances also offer senior seating with tickets costing $2.

AGE: 65
COST: $5 or $2 (see above)
PHONE: 806-376-8782
INTERNET: http://www.actx.edu/~symphony
              (Web page)
              symphony@arn.net (e-mail)

THE AUSTIN SYMPHONY

The Austin Symphony was founded in 1911 and is Austin's oldest performing arts group. The Symphony offers performances in the Bass Concert Hall on the University of Texas campus and in Palmer Auditorium. Performances are at 8:00 p.m. Fridays and Saturdays during the season.

AGE: 62
DISCOUNT: $2 off
PHONE: 888-4-MAESTRO (888-462-3787)
INTERNET: http://quadralay.com.arts.aso.html

FORT WORTH SYMPHONY ORCHESTRA*

The Fort Worth Symphony offers a 30% discount to seniors, full-time students, and full-time teachers for Masterpiece and Virtuoso performances, but not for Pops performances. The Fort Worth Symphony Orchestra will celebrate a new home in 1988 at the newly constructed Nancy Lee and Perry R. Bass Performance Hall.

AGE: 65
DISCOUNT: 30%
PHONE: 817-926-8831

HOUSTON SYMPHONY ORCHESTRA

Enjoy the Houston Symphony with a senior discount.

AGE: 65
COST: $5 per person
ADDRESS: Jones Hall
              615 Louisiana
PHONE: 800-828-ARTS

Tickets must be purchased in person one-half hour prior to curtain at the street level box office at Jones Hall. Each purchaser must show a photo identification showing his or her birth date (i.e., one ID per person). These tickets are subject to availability and are not available for Exxon Pops Concerts, galas, or special events.

---

* (Source: *The Excitement is Building . . .*, Fort Worth Symphony Orchestra)

Restaurants and Fast Food

RESTAURANTS

BOB'S CATFISH-N-MORE

You'll find a menu filled with catfish, shrimp, stuffed crab, and all kinds of chicken at this Georgetown restaurant. They serve lunch from 11:00 a.m. to 2:00 p.m. and dinner from 5:00 p.m. to 8:30 p.m. Bob's Catfish-n-More is closed Sundays.

AGE:	55
DISCOUNT:	Senior Plate
ADDRESS:	305 E. Morrow
	Georgetown
PHONE:	512-863-6219

BUSY BEE CAFE

For country-style cooking in a cozy atmosphere, you'll enjoy the Busy Bee Cafe, a Texas tradition since 1935.

AGE:	60
DISCOUNT:	Order from the Senior Menu or 15% off regular menu (except the sandwich menu)
ADDRESSES:	**Alvin**
	2417 S. Gordon
	281-331-2298

Pearland
4009 W. Broadway
281-485-8690
Santa Fe
12350 Hwy. 6
409-925-3156
Texas City
3440 Palmer Hwy.
713-945-8444

COUNTY LINE

The County Line restaurants serve some of the best barbecue in Texas in a pleasant, rustic atmosphere. They are located in Austin, Corpus Christi, El Paso, Houston, Lubbock, and San Antonio.

AGE: 55 (or at the Manager's discretion)
DISCOUNT: Order off the child's menu or a la carte

DENNY'S*

Serving hungry travelers since 1953, Denny's are open 24 hours a day from Maine to California and from Amarillo to McAllen. Consult the Index at the end of this book for a listing of cities with Denny's locations.

AGE: 55
DISCOUNT: Order from Senior Citizen Menu

You can pick up a *Denny's Travel Directory* at most restaurants that will detail their locations and highway exits across the country.

---

* (Source: *Denny's Travel Directory,* Denny's)

EL PALACIO

When you're visiting Sun City in Georgetown, be sure to stop in El Palacio for some great Mexican food. If it's your birthday, you'll receive a sopapilla with a candle while the mariachis serenade you. They're open Thursdays through Saturdays from 11:15 a.m. to 9:00 p.m. and offer a Sunday buffet from 11:30 a.m. to 2:00 p.m.

AGE:	60
DISCOUNT:	10%
ADDRESS:	1201 Church St.
	Georgetown
PHONE:	512-869-4100

FURR'S CAFETERIA*

Since 1947, Furr's Cafeterias of Lubbock have served up good food with reasonable prices and friendly service. Now you can get all that with a senior discount at all their other locations across Texas, too.

AGE:	55
DISCOUNT:	50 cents off regular lunch and dinner buffet

Furr's also offers a lite plate on Saturday and Sunday with a senior discount of 30 cents off the regular price ($4.35 for seniors). Just fill out an application for a senior discount card at your local Furr's Cafeteria.

When you visit Furr's Cafeteria, pick up one of their directories that lists the addresses for all their locations across the country.

GOLDEN CORRAL RESTAURANTS

The Golden Corral restaurants offer a buffet of meat and vegetable entrées, salad, fruit, and fresh baked goods. Corporate-

---

* (Source: *Wherever You Travel, Come Home to Furr's,* Furr's/Bishop's, Inc.)

owned Golden Corral restaurants offer the following discount, but some franchise restaurants may not. Check the restaurant near you for their senior policy.

AGE: 65
DISCOUNT: 50 cents off buffet price

INTERNATIONAL HOUSE OF PANCAKES (IHOP) RESTAURANTS*

Senior programs may vary at the IHOPs, but many offer the Golden Age Club that gives seniors a 10% discount off the regular menu. Some of the IHOPs also have an "early bird special" from 3 to 6 p.m. Call your local IHOP for details.

AGE: 55
DISCOUNT: 10% at participating locations only

LITTLE RIVER CAFE

Order breakfast, lunch, or dinner at this cafe located in the La Quinta Inn in Georgetown. Sundays through Fridays they also offer a lunch buffet.

AGE: 50
DISCOUNT: 10%
ADDRESS: 333 North IH-35
                     Georgetown
PHONE: 512-869-2541

LONE STAR CAFE

Visit the Lone Star Cafe for some great chicken-fried steak and more. You'll have some fun down at the Lone Star Cafe. Lone Star Cafes are located in Austin, Hillsboro, Round Rock, and San Marcos.

---

* (Source: *Our Location Guide,* International House of Pancakes)

AGE: 55
DISCOUNT: Senior menu

MESA HILLS CAFE

This Austin Hill Country cafe offers a variety of foods such as Tex-Mex, chicken Caesar salad, seafood, and sandwiches. Their Sunday brunch will delight you with both European and Western dishes and a variety of salads and omelets.

Mesa Hills Cafe's "Senior Citizen Social Club" receives my top honors for Texas restaurants. Fill out a Senior Citizen Registration Card and enjoy this charming cafe. For seniors 59 and older, they offer the following benefits:

- 20% discount on the meal price anytime
- 50% discount on their Sunday Brunch
- $2 for dessert and coffee or tea every day from 2 to 4 p.m.
- Complimentary dessert and glass of wine with your entrée on your birthday
- 25% discount on a gift certificate of $10 or $25

ADDRESS: 3435 Greystone
              Austin
PHONE: 512-345-7423

MR. GATTI'S

Mr. Gatti's restaurants offer a lunch and dinner buffet including pizza, spaghetti, salad, and dessert. The corporate Mr. Gatti's restaurants offer the following senior discount. The franchise restaurants may offer a different discount or no discount. Please call the Mr. Gatti's in your area for their senior citizen program.

AGE: 55
DISCOUNT: 50 cents off the buffet

OLD SAN FRANCISCO STEAK HOUSE

The girl in the red velvet swing and great food are waiting for you at the Old San Francisco Steak House. This restaurant has locations in Austin, Dallas, Houston, and San Antonio.

AGE: 55
DISCOUNT: 25% off entrées anytime

PIT BARBECUE

RANCH HOUSE BARBECUE

When you're in the mood for barbecue, visit the Pit Barbecue or the Ranch House Barbecue in Georgetown. They both have great food and offer slightly different discounts.

AGE: 55 (Pit Barbecue), 65 (Ranch House
                    Barbecue)
DISCOUNT: 10% (Pit Barbecue), 15% dine-in orders only
                    (Ranch House Barbecue)
ADDRESSES: **Pit Barbecue**
                    2427 Williams Dr.
                    Georgetown
                    512-863-9083
                    Ranch House Barbecue
                    301 Leander Rd.
                    Georgetown
                    512-863-2299

SHONEY'S RESTAURANTS*

You'll find good food in comfortable surroundings at a near-by Shoney's Restaurant. This is a full-service restaurant, and many locations have a breakfast bar until 11:00 a.m. This discount is only at participating restaurants. Call for details.

*(Source: *Road Atlas & Directory*, Shoney's, Inc.)

```
AGE:        55
DISCOUNT:   50 cents off complete meals
PHONE:      800-222-2222
```

SIRLOIN STOCKADE*

Sirloin Stockade's commitment to their customers is:

- Steaks cut daily in their restaurants
- No preservatives used
- Freshly prepared buffet items they cook themselves
- Friendly service and great value
- 100% satisfaction guaranteed

The senior discount may vary with the restaurant, so please call the restaurant near you for details. Sirloin Stockade restaurants are located in several Texas cities. Consult the Index at the back of this book for a location near you.

```
AGE:        55
DISCOUNT:   10%
PHONE:      316-669-9372
```

STEAK AND ALE

Dine at a Steak and Ale restaurant and enjoy their "Early Evenings" special seven days a week. You'll be able to choose from their complete specially priced dinners, including the salad bar or Caesar salad, entrée with bread, non-alcoholic beverage, and dessert for one discounted price. Their early evening prices are available Monday–Friday: 4–6 p.m.; Saturday: 2–5 p.m.: and Sunday: 11:30 a.m.–5 p.m. There is no age requirement for these prices. Note, however, Early Evenings meals are not available on

---

* (Source: *The Sirloin Stockade Concept and Sirloin Stockade Locations Guide,* Sirloin Stockade International)

Mother's Day, Father's Day, Valentine's Day, Thanksgiving, Christmas, New Year's Eve, or other designated holidays.

TACO CABANA

Taco Cabana serves good Tex-Mex food with a south-of-the-border flair. This discount may not be available at all Taco Cabanas, so please check first.

AGE: 55
DISCOUNT: 10%

THE BIG TEXAN STEAK RANCH*

Dine in an atmosphere of old west decor and eat a Cowboy Poet's Breakfast or a 72-ounce steak at this Amarillo restaurant in The Big Texan Inn. You might also want to take a look at their Texas-shaped heated pool.

AGE: 55
DISCOUNT: Order from the Senior Menu section
ADDRESS: 7701 I-40 East
                 Amarillo
PHONE: 806-372-5000

THE OLD ALLIGATOR GRILL

This is where you'll find wonderful New Orleans-style cooking in Austin.

AGE: 65
DISCOUNT: 10% off, except alcoholic beverages (not
                 valid with any other discounts or coupons)
ADDRESS: 3003 S. Lamar
                 Austin
PHONE: 512-444-6117

---

* (Source: Internet: http://www.amarillo-cyborg/hotels.html)

WAFFLE HOUSE

Waffle House restaurants are located in many small towns and along the interstates of Texas. Enjoy breakfast, sandwich plates, hamburgers, and dinner plates in this Georgia-based family restaurant. Most franchises offer the following senior discount, but be sure to ask.

AGE: 60
DISCOUNT: 10%

FAST FOOD

GENERAL GUIDELINES

Most of these restaurants are franchises, and their senior discount programs may vary within the chain. Please consult your telephone directory for a location near you.

ARBY'S ROAST BEEF SANDWICH
AGE: 55
DISCOUNT: Free coffee and soft drinks with meal

CAPTAIN D'S
AGE: 55
DISCOUNT: 10%

DAIRY QUEEN
AGE: 55
DISCOUNT: 10%

GOLDEN FRIED CHICKEN
AGE: 55
DISCOUNT: 10% off individual meals

HARDEES
AGE: 55
DISCOUNT: 10% with Hardees Advantage Club Card

JACK IN THE BOX

AGE: 55
DISCOUNT: All drinks 25 cents

KENTUCKY FRIED CHICKEN (KFC)

AGE: 65
DISCOUNT: 10%

LONG JOHN SILVER'S SEAFOOD SHOPPE

AGE: 55
DISCOUNT: 10%

McDONALD'S RESTAURANT

AGE: 55 (Ask for a Senior Discount Card)
DISCOUNT: All small drinks 25 cents

PIZZA HUT

AGE: 65
DISCOUNT: 10% to 15%

POPEYES FAMOUS FRIED CHICKEN & BISCUITS

AGE: 55
DISCOUNT: 10%

TACO BUENO

AGE: 55
DISCOUNT: 10% (Seniors must ask for discount)

WENDY'S OLD FASHIONED HAMBURGERS

AGE: 60
DISCOUNT: 10% off everything and free drink refills

WHATABURGER

AGE: 55
DISCOUNT: Club 55 Card—small drink or coffee free
                     with burger

Senior
Organizations

AARP*

Even if you're nowhere near retirement, you're still eligible to join the American Association of Retired Persons (AARP) when you turn 50. About 35 million members strong, AARP offers members a variety of discounts, and it is one of the most effective lobbying groups in Washington.

AGE: 50
ADDRESS: **Texas State Office**
           Nancy Snead, State Representative
           98 San Jacinto Blvd., Ste. 750
           Austin, Texas 78701
PHONE: 512-480-9797
           800-424-3410

AARP is widely recognized. A significant benefit of having an AARP membership card is getting a senior discount at 50 when a business usually designates its discounts for those 55 or older. This alone is worth the $8 membership fee when you turn 50. Your membership fee buys, among other things, the following:

- Travel discounts on lodging and car rentals
- *Modern Maturity* magazine and the *Bulletin* newspaper

---

* (Source: *AARP in Texas* and *Sign Up to be an AARP Member Today!*, American Association of Retired Persons)

- Home-delivery pharmacy
- Legislative advocacy on important issues
- Free membership for your spouse
- Free information-packed guidebooks
- Auto, home, life, and health insurance

AARP Texas currently has about 1.9 million members with 392 Texas chapters and 227 Texas Retired Teacher Units.

AARP in Texas has the following programs. Call your local AARP chapter for more details.

- Health Advocacy Services
- 55 Alive/Mature Driving Program
- State Legislative Committee
- Capital City Task Force
- AARP/Vote
- Connections for Independent Living
- Minority Affairs
- Tax-Aide
- Retired Teachers Association
- Widowed Persons Service
- Work Force Programs
- Women's Initiative
- Women's Financial Information Project
- Legal Hotline for Older Texans—800-622-2520

SEARS—MATURE OUTLOOK*

Sears—Mature Outlook is a membership program for seniors 50 and up that costs $19.95 per year. Call the toll-free number for information or enrollment. Gift memberships are available.

---

* (Source: *Expand Your Horizons with Mature Outlook,* Sears)

AGE: 50
COST: $19.95 per year
PHONE: 800-336-6330

Benefits of Mature Outlook include:

- $100 in Sears Money Coupons, good at any Sears store, any day of the week, on both regular and sale-priced merchandise
- Members-only discounts from the Sears Optical Department
- *Mature Outlook* magazine from the publishers of *Better Homes and Gardens*
- 50% discount at over 2,600 participating hotels
- Discount dining can save you up to 20% at over 1,000 restaurants
- Car rental discounts from National, Avis, Hertz, Alamo, and Sears/Budget
- No-fee CitiCorp Travelers Checks and a free Social Security earnings request form

Senior Friends *

Senior Friends is a national healthcare-based organization for adults 50 and better. There are approximately 222 chapters in the country, all sponsored by Columbia Health Care, with more than 280,000 members. A one-year membership is $15.

A list of the Columbia Health Care Facilities was not available from either Senior Friends or Columbia Health Care; however, when you dial the Columbia toll-free number, your call is automatically routed to the Columbia facility closest to you. You may also check your local phone directory for a Columbia Health Care provider in your area.

---

* (Source: *Providing Healthy Options for Happier Living,* National Association of Senior Friends)

AGE: 50
COST: $15 per year
PHONE: 800-348-4886
            800-COLUMBIA

The Senior Friends national discount program includes:

- Prescriptions
- Retirement and financial planning
- Vision and hearing care
- Hotel accommodations and car rentals
- Appliance service contracts
- Hardcover books up to 70% off
- International/domestic travel

If you're admitted to a participating Columbia/HCA hospital, your VIP hospital privileges may include:

- VIP hospital privileges
- Complimentary meal plan for spouse or caregiver
- Room upgrades when available
- Member cafeteria discount

Benefits that may be offered by your local chapter include:

- Free assistance in filing health insurance and Medicare claims
- Free notary and photocopy services
- Free or discounted health screenings, seminars, and lectures
- Social activities, such as: lunch clubs, mall walking, aerobics, games, getaways, sporting events, and volunteer opportunities

SILVER WINGS PLUS*

United Airlines offers its Silver Wings Plus discount program for travelers age 60 and better. The cost for a three-year mem-

---

* (Source: *Big Savings for Travelers Age 62 Plus,* United Airlines)

bership is $75 or $150 for a lifetime membership. With the three-year membership, you receive three $25 Discount Certificates good for United flights or toward the purchase of United Silver TravelPac Coupons (see Chapter 1, Airlines and Car Rental). With a lifetime membership, you'll receive three $50 certificates.

Members age 62 and up receive a full 10% off selected published airfares to most domestic and international destinations on United, United Express, and other international air travel partners. You'll also enjoy discounts from 10% to 50% at:

- Westin Hotels and Resorts
- Radisson Hotels International
- Hyatt Hotels and Resorts
- Choice Hotels International

Silver Wings Plus members can take advantage of special cruise packages on Holland America Line and Royal Caribbean Cruise Line. In addition, as a Silver Wings Plus member, you'll automatically receive United Mileage Plus Frequent Flyer Miles for free flights and upgrades. When you join with a three-year membership, you receive 1,500 Mileage Plus bonus miles and 3,000 miles for a lifetime membership.

Texas Department on Aging

The mission of the Texas Department on Aging is to be "the state's visible advocate and leader in providing for a comprehensive and coordinated continuum of services and opportunities so that older people can live dignified, independent, and productive lives."

To complete their mission, this state agency has set up Area Agencies on Aging offices across the state to provide older Texans with:

- Information and assistance
- Benefits counseling

- Case management
- Ombudsman services (State Nursing Home Ombudsman: 800-252-2412)

They have created an intriguing profile of the Texas senior population you may want to request called *Older Texans Today—A Thumbnail Sketch*. Using 1994 U.S. Census Bureau statistics, they report that of the approximately 18 million people in Texas, 2.5 million (about 14%) are at least 60 years of age. They also state the Texan 60-and-older population is growing faster than the general population.

This interesting article also discusses older Texans relative to rural issues, health status, and impairment levels, cultural diversity, financial status, housing, and transportation. For a free copy, contact your local Area Agency on Aging or:

The Texas Department on Aging

4900 N. Lamar
Austin, TX 78741
512-424-6840
800-252-9240
Internet: http://www.texas.gov/agency/340.html (e-mail)

AREA AGENCIES ON AGING*

Abilene

West Central Texas Area Agency on Aging
1025 E. North 10th St.
915-672-8544
800-928-2262
Counties Served:
Brown, Callahan, Coleman, Comanche, Eastland, Fisher, Haskell, Jones, Kent, Knox, Mitchell, Nolan, Runnels, Scurry, Shackelford, Stephens, Stonewall, Taylor, and Throckmorton

---

* (Source: *Area Agencies on Aging Directory of Access and Assistance,* Texas Department on Aging)

Amarillo

Panhandle Area Agency on Aging
415 W. 8th
806-372-3381
800-642-6008
Counties Served:
Armstrong, Briscoe, Carson, Castro, Childress, Collingsworth,
Dallam, Deaf Smith, Donley, Gray, Hall, Hansford, Hartley,
Hemphill, Hutchinson, Lipscomb, Moore, Ochiltree,
Oldham, Parmer, Potter, Randall, Roberts, Sherman, Swisher,
and Wheeler

Arlington

North Central Texas Area Agency on Aging
616 Six Flags Drive
817-695-9194
800-272-3921
Counties Served:
Collin, Denton, Ellis, Erath, Hood, Hunt, Johnson, Kaufman,
Navarro, Palo Pinto, Parker, Rockwall, Somervell, and Wise

Austin

Capital Area Agency on Aging
2520 S. IH 35, Ste. 100
512-443-7653 (Collect calls accepted)
Counties Served:
Bastrop, Blanco, Burnet, Caldwell, Fayette, Hays, Lee, Llano,
Travis, and Williamson

Family Eldercare, Inc. is also an excellent resource for information in the Austin area. This organization provides information and referral for older Texans, and they also produce the very useful *Travis County Guide to Services for Older Adults*. Individuals, organizations, and libraries may purchase this book for $26. If your Travis County library doesn't have a copy, urge them to contact Family Eldercare at:

Family Eldercare, Inc.
3710 Cedar St., Ste. 225
Austin, TX 78705
512-450-0844

Belton

Central Texas Area Agency on Aging
302 E. Central
817-939-1886
800-447-7169
Counties Served:
  Bell, Coryell, Hamilton, Lampassas, Milam, Mills,
  and San Saba

Bryan

Brazos Valley Area Agency on Aging
1706 E. 29th St.
409-775-4244
800-994-4000
Counties Served:
  Brazos, Burleson, Grimes, Leon, Madison, Robertson,
  and Washington

Carrizo Springs

Middle Rio Grande Area Agency on Aging
307 W. Nopal St.
210-876-3533
800-224-4262
Counties Served:
  Dimmit, Edwards, Kinney, LaSalle, Maverick, Real, Uvalde,
  Val Verde, and Zavala

Corpus Christi

Coastal Bend Area Agency on Aging
2910 Leopard
512-883-5743
800-817-5743 (Statewide)
Counties Served:
  Aransas, Bee, Brooks, Duval, Jim Wells, Kenedy, Kleberg, Live
  Oak, McMullen, Nueces, Refugio, and San Patricio

Dallas

Dallas County Area Agency on Aging
2121 Main St., Ste. 500
214-871-5065
County Served: Dallas

El Paso

Rio Grande Area Agency on Aging
1100 N. Stanton, Ste. 610
915-533-0998
800-333-7082
Counties Served:
   Brewster, Culberson, El Paso, Hudspeth, Jeff Davis,
   and Presidio

Fort Worth

Tarrant County Area Agency on Aging
210 E. Ninth St.
817-258-8081
County Served: Tarrant

Houston

Harris County Area Agency on Aging
8000 N. Stadium Dr., 3rd floor
713-794-9001
800-213-8471 (National)
County Served: Harris

Houston-Galveston

Houston-Galveston Area Agency on Aging
3555 Timmons Ln., Ste. 500
713-627-3200
800-437-7396
Counties Served:
   Austin, Brazoria, Chambers, Colorado, Fort Bend, Galveston,
   Liberty, Matagorda, Montgomery, Walker, Waller, and Wharton

Jasper

Deep East Texas Area Agency on Aging
274 E. Lamar
409-384-5704
800-435-3377 (National)
Counties Served:
   Angelina, Houston, Jasper, Nacogdoches, Newton, Polk,
   Sabine, San Augustine, San Jacinto, Shelby, Trinity, and Tyler

Kilgore

East Texas Area Agency on Aging
3800 Stone Rd.
903-984-8641
800-442-8845
Counties Served:
Anderson, Camp, Cherokee, Gregg, Harrison, Henderson, Marion, Panola, Rains, Rusk, Smith, Upshur, Van Zandt, and Wood

Laredo

South Texas Area Agency on Aging
1718 E. Calton Rd.
210-722-3995
800-292-5426
Counties Served:
Jim Hogg, Starr, Webb, and Zapata

Lubbock

South Plains Area Agency on Aging
1323 58th St.
806-762-8721
800-858-1809
Counties Served:
Bailey, Cochran, Crosby, Dickens, Floyd, Garza, Hall, Hockley, King, Lamb, Lubbock, Lynn, Motley, Terry, and Yoakum

McAllen

Lower Rio Grande Valley Area Agency on Aging
311 N. 15th St.
210-682-3481
800-365-6131 (National)
Counties Served:
Cameron, Hidalgo, and Willacy

Midland

Permian Basin Area Agency on Aging
2910 LaForce Blvd.
915-563-1061
800-491-4636
Counties Served:
   Andrews, Borden, Crane, Dawson, Ector, Gaines, Glasscock,
   Howard, Loving, Martin, Midland, Pecos, Reeves, Terrell,
   Upton, Ward, and Winkler

Port Arthur

South East Texas Area Agency on Aging
3501 Turtle Creek Dr., Ste. 108
409-727-2384
800-395-5465
Counties Served:
   Hardin, Jefferson, and Orange

San Angelo

Concho Valley Area Agency on Aging
5002 Knickerbocker
915-944-9666
800-728-2592
Counties Served:
   Coke, Concho, Crockett, Irion, Kimble, Mason, McCulloch,
   Menard, Reagan, Schleicher, Sterling, Sutton, and Tom Green

San Antonio

Alamo Area Agency on Aging
118 Broadway, Ste. 400
210-225-5201
800-960-5201
Counties Served:
   Atascosa, Bandera, Comal, Frio, Gillespie, Guadalupe, Karnes,
   Kendall, Kerr, Medina, and Wilson

Bexar County Area Agency on Aging
118 Broadway, Ste. 400
210-225-5201
800-960-5201
County Served: Bexar

Sherman

Texoma Area Agency on Aging
3201 Texoma Pkwy., Ste. 220
903-813-3581 or
903-813-3505
800-677-8264
Counties Served:
  Cooke, Fannin, and Grayson

Victoria

Golden Crescent Area Agency on Aging
568 Big Bend Drive
512-578-1587
800-574-9745
Counties Served:
  Calhoun, DeWitt, Goliad, Gonzales, Jackson, Lavaca, and Victoria

Waco

Heart of Texas Area Agency on Aging
300 Franklin Ave.
817-756-7822
800-460-2121
Counties Served:
  Bosque, Falls, Freestone, Hill, Limestone, and McLennan

Wake Village

Ark-Tex Area Agency on Aging
911 N. Bishop Rd.
903-832-8785
800-372-4464
Counties Served:
  Bowie, Cass, Delta, Franklin, Hopkins, Lamar, Morris, Red
  River, and Titus

Wichita Falls

North Texas Area Agency on Aging
4309 Jacksboro Hwy.
817-322-5281
800-460-2226
Counties Served:
  Archer, Baylor, Clay, Cottle, Foard, Hardeman, Jack, Montague,
  Wichita, Wilbarger, and Young

Shopping

DEPARTMENT STORES

BEALLS DEPARTMENT STORE

This department store sells clothes, accessories, and gift items. They also offer the best department-store-senior program I found in the state.

AGE: 55
DISCOUNT: 20% off regular and sale merchandise on the first Tuesday of the month

If you open a Bealls charge account on the first Tuesday of the month, you may take an additional 10% off whatever you purchase.

On their "Senior Tuesday" mornings, Bealls usually serves free juice or coffee and cookies. Bealls will often arrange to have health care professionals in to do free blood sugar analyses, blood pressure checks, and similar services for seniors.

J. C. PENNEY

Houston is the only city in Texas where the J. C. Penney Company offers a senior discount, and they have plans to phase this program out entirely in Texas. Currently, Houston stores offer the following program.

AGE: 55
DISCOUNT: 15% (second Tuesday of the month)

RESTRICTIONS: No discount on cosmetics, catalog
items, custom decorating
10% discount on furniture

MONTGOMERY WARD*

Montgomery Ward has a program called the Y.E.S. Discount
Club that costs $34.95 a year (or $2.99 a month). With Y.E.S.
(Years of Extra Savings), seniors 55 and over get a 10% discount
every Tuesday on all regular or sale-priced merchandise at any
Montgomery Ward store.

```
AGE:          55
DISCOUNT:     10% every Tuesday
PHONE:        800-421-5396
```

This discount is on major appliances, home furnishings, elec-
tronics, jewelry, apparel, gift items, labor charges on auto services, etc. In addition, this program includes a Y.E.S. Club
Travel Service on tours, cruises, hotels, and car rental.

The 10% Tuesday discount may not be used in conjunction
with any other discount or coupon. It's not valid for sales tax,
delivery, service contracts, or Montgomery Ward Clearance
Outlet Center. Your local Montgomery Ward Store can give you
a brochure and take your application.

PALAIS ROYAL

Palais Royal stores and Bealls Department Stores are both
owned by Stage Management, Inc. They sell clothes, accessories,
and gift items.

```
AGE:          55
DISCOUNT:     20% off regular and sale merchandise on
              first Tuesday of the month
```

---

* (Source: *Montgomery Ward Y.E.S. Discount Club,* Montgomery Ward)

If you happen to open a Palais Royal charge account on the first Tuesday of the month, you may take an additional 10% off whatever you purchase. On their "Senior Tuesday" mornings, Palais Royal often serves free juice or coffee and cookies. They will often arrange to have health care professionals in to do free blood sugar analyses, blood pressure checks, and similar services for the seniors.

ROSS DRESS FOR LESS

This store has designer labels at discounted prices on men's, women's, and children's clothes, shoes, and accessories.

AGE: 55 up
DISCOUNT: 10% on Tuesdays

SEARS*

Sears offers a membership program for seniors 50 and older that costs $19.95 per year and offers the following benefits. Call the toll-free number for information or enrollment. Gift memberships are available.

AGE: 50
COST: $19.95 per year
PHONE: 800-336-6330

Benefits include:

- $100 in Sears Money coupons good at any Sears store, any day of the week, on both regular and sale-priced merchandise
- Members-only discounts from the Sears Optical Department
- *Mature Outlook* magazine from the publishers of *Better Homes and Gardens*
- 50% discount at over 2,600 participating hotels

---

* (Source: *Expand Your Horizons with Mature Outlook*, Sears)

- Discount dining can save you up to 20% at over 1,000 restaurants
- Car rental discounts from National, Avis, Hertz, Alamo, and Sears/Budget
- No-fee CitiCorp travelers checks and a free Social Security earnings request form

WEINER'S STORES INC.

Weiner's Stores are a great place to find mid-priced and bargain clothes for men, women, and children. Approximately once a month, they'll advertise a senior day and take 10% off everything in the store (including sale items) for seniors.

AGE: 55
DISCOUNT: 10% off everything only on advertised days

The advertisement promoting their senior discount day will appear in circulars in local newspapers and will be advertised on radio and television. In addition, most stores use a pedestal sign to announce the store's next senior day sale.

BOOKSTORES

B. DALTON BOOKSELLER

B. Dalton doesn't offer a senior discount, but they do have lots of other good discounts:

- 25% discount on B. Dalton's top ten hardcover best sellers
- Book Savers Card ($10/year) gives a 10% discount off everything (except magazines and gift certificates). This discount can be used on top of the 25% discount mentioned above and on other discounted items.
- Corporate Discount program for corporations, institutions, schools, libraries, civic groups, etc., when you complete an application and present an approved purchase order:

15% off purchases of $10–$999
20% off purchases of $1,000–$4,999
25% off purchases of $5,000+

BARNES & NOBLE

Barnes & Noble have been booksellers since 1873, and they offer the following discounts to all patrons.

Quantity Discounts on single purchases of a hardcover or paperback title:*

20% off 30–249 copies
25% off 250–999 copies
1,000 copies or more. Call them to negotiate.

Educator's Discounts are offered to all teachers and educators of grades Pre K–12. Bring your valid school ID or pay stub to pick up an Educator's Discount Card the next time you're in the store. You'll receive 20% off the publisher's list price on a single purchase of hardcover or paperback titles for use in the classroom.

Nonprofit Discounts are offered to institutions, libraries, schools, civic groups, or nonprofit organizations (senior centers). Bring your not-for-profit tax-exemption certificate with you to receive these discounts on a single purchase of hardcover or paperback titles:*

20% off purchases of $1–$999
25% off purchases of $1,000 or more

Corporate Discounts are offered to corporations or businesses on a single purchase of hardcover or paperback titles:*

20% off purchases of $100–$999
25% off purchases of $1,000 or more

* All discounts are off the publisher's list price. Discounts not available on textbooks, periodicals, CDs, multimedia, cassettes, and other non-book merchandise. Discounts are subject to change without notice and may vary on some special orders.

BOOK PEOPLE

This one-of-a-kind bookstore in Austin offers some great discounts on books.

- 10% discount on hardcover books (they have a large bargain book section)
- 30% discount on Staff Selections of hardcover and paperback books
- 30% discount on *New York Times* bestseller hardcover books
- Quantity discounts: 10–24 = 15%
                         25–49 = 20%
                         100+ = negotiable
- 10% discount on books used in the classroom and purchased by K–12 teachers

ADDRESS:	603 N. Lamar
	Austin
PHONE:	512-472-5050

BOOKSOURCE

If you're searching for a special-order book or just want to find some great fiction, visit the Booksource in Austin. The Research Blvd. location is a "general reader" store with lots of fiction. The South Lamar location also carries toys and has a music department with records, CDs, cassettes, and posters. The Booksource stores are currently the only bookstores in Austin offering a senior discount.

AGE:	55
DISCOUNT:	10%
ADDRESSES:	13729 Research Blvd.
	Austin
	512-258-1313
	Westgate Mall
	4543 S. Lamar
	512-891-9588

BOOKSTOP

Bookstop stores are owned by the same corporation as Barnes & Noble, but they have a slightly different discount structure with their Readers Choice discount card. These discounts are offered to all patrons.

Everyday discounts of 10% on every hardcover and paperback book and 25% on current *New York Times* hardcover bestsellers.

Readers Choice Discount Cards cost $9 per year and offer discounts of:

- 20% off every hardcover book except textbooks and bargain books
- 10% off newspapers and magazines
- 20% off all paperback books
- 40% off current *New York Times* hardcover bestsellers

Quantity Discounts on single purchases of hardcover or paperback titles*:

- 20% off 30–249 copies
- 25% off 250–999 copies
- 1,000 copies or more. Call them to negotiate.

Educator's Discounts are offered to all teachers and educators of grades Pre K–12. Bring your valid school ID or pay stub to pick up an Educator's Discount Card the next time you're in the store. You'll receive 20% off the publisher's list price on a single purchase of hardcover or paperback titles for use in the classroom.

Nonprofit Discounts are offered to institutions, libraries, schools, civic groups, or nonprofit organizations (senior centers). Bring your not-for-profit tax-exemption certificate with you to receive these discounts on a single purchase of hardcover or paperback titles*:

- 20% off purchases of $1–$999
- 25% off purchases of $1,000 or more

Corporate Discounts are offered to corporations or businesses on a single purchase of hardcover or paperback titles*:

- 20% off purchases of $100–$999
- 25% off purchases of $1,000 or more
- * All discounts are off the publisher's list price. Discounts are not available on textbooks, periodicals, CDs, multimedia, cassettes, and other non-book merchandise. Discounts are subject to change without notice and may vary on some special orders.

BORDERS BOOKS AND MUSIC

Borders began in 1971 when Tom and Louis Borders opened a "serious" bookshop in the heart of Ann Arbor's academic community. From those humble beginnings, Borders has grown to support stores with a company-wide title base of over 200,000 books, music, and new media titles. Their discounts are listed below and are not available on non-stock special orders or periodicals. They may not be combined with promotional or special discounts.

Quantity Discount. All customers are eligible for the following discounts on a single purchase:

- 10% for 10–19 copies of a single paperback title
- 15% for 10–19 copies of a single hardcover title
- 15% for 20–29 copies of a single title
- 20% for 30 or more copies of a single title

Nonprofit Discount. Nonprofit organizations with a federal tax exempt number receive 20% off the publisher's list price for book, music, and video merchandise.

Classroom Discount. Borders offers 20% off the publisher's list price to K–12 teachers and librarians for book, music, and video merchandise for student use in the classroom or library.

Volume Discount. Institutions and businesses that are house accounts (ask for a House Account application form) receive the following discounts on single purchases:

- 15% discount on purchase of $25–$499.99
- 20% discount on purchase of $500–$4,999.99
- 25% discount on purchase of $5,000 or more

CROWN BOOKS

Crown Books of Landover, Maryland, operates both Crown Books and Super Crown Books in Texas. They sell books, puzzles, games, CDs, software, greeting cards, eye glasses, and much more. They're expanding their locations in Texas and are currently located in Clear Lake, Dallas, Houston, and Humble. Their discounts include the following:

- 15% discount on all hardcover books
- 10% discount on all softcover books
- 40% discount on *New York Times* Bestseller hardcover books
- 25% discount on *New York Times* Bestseller softcover books
- Additional 5% discount for all teachers buying books for classroom use

WALDENBOOKS*

Like most other bookstores, Waldenbooks doesn't offer a senior discount, but they do have plenty of other discounts:

- 25% discount on their Hardcover Bestseller List. This list changes weekly and is based on their nationwide sales.

* (Source: *How to Save Even More . . . Become a Waldenbooks Preferred Reader Today!*, Waldenbooks)

- **Preferred Reader Card ($10/year).** Ten percent discount on everything and accrue one point for every dollar spent. When you have accrued 100 points, you receive a $5 gift certificate in the mail. Points are accrued on the retail price, before tax. Preferred Readers also may use a toll-free number, 800-322-2000, Dept. 400, and still get their 10% discount to a) place an order, b) send a present gift-wrapped with a personal message, or c) ask about locating a special book you can't find. You can also use this toll-free number to apply for your Preferred Reader Card.

- **Wise Corporate Account Card.** Quantity discounts for corporations, schools, hospitals, libraries, civic groups, and other organizations on books and audio cassettes:

  - 15% discount on purchase of $25–$1,000
  - 20% discount on purchase of $1,001–$5,000
  - 25% discount on purchase of $5,001 or more

For qualifying nonprofit organizations, discount per purchase are as follows:

- 20% discount on purchase of $25–$5,000
- 25% discount on purchase of $5,001 or more

NOTE: Magazines, gift certificates, and some technical/reference books do not qualify for the discount. Corporate discounts cannot be combined with any other discounts.

CHILDREN'S STORES

LIL' THINGS

If you're looking for that perfect baby gift, look no further than Lil' Things, and you'll get a senior discount. They carry infant and toddler clothes, furniture, toys, and gifts. Lil' Things is located in Arlington, Austin, Houston, Lewisville, Mesquite, and Plano.

AGE: 50
DISCOUNT: 10% Tuesdays

COSMETICS

BEAUTICONTROL COSMETICS, INC.

Beauty consultant Evelyn Aubrey Case offers a 15% discount on all products purchased from her in your birth month. When you pick up your order from her in Austin, she also offers seniors regular discounts based on your age. Special arrangements can be made for those unable to pick up the products and for those persons in other parts of the state.

AGE: 50
DISCOUNT: 10% off all products
AGE: 60
DISCOUNT: 15% off all products
AGE: 70 and better
DISCOUNT: 20% off all products
PHONE: 512-219-0606 (in Austin calling area)
              800-280-2360 (outside Austin calling area)

BeautiControl has a respected line of personal care products in the following areas:

- Skin care
- Makeup
- Hair products
- Nail care
- Cortisone-based skin products

- Weight loss management
- Nutrition supplements
- Food supplements
- Aroma therapy

CRAFTS

HANDCRAFTS UNLIMITED

This unique shop in Georgetown is a great place to shop as well as a great place for seniors to sell their handcrafted wares. This nonprofit store requires all of its Williamson County contributing artisans be 50 years or better. This is a great place to put that "artsy" hobby of yours to work for you!

ADDRESS: 104 W. 8th St.
            Georgetown
PHONE: 512-863-3072

MICHAELS—THE ARTS AND CRAFTS STORE

This store has almost everything you would ever need for arts and crafts—from dried flowers to picture frames.

AGE: 55
DISCOUNT: 10% off regular prices before noon

MOSKALEIS

For your arts and crafts supplies in Grapevine, visit Moskaleis.

AGE: 55
DISCOUNT: 10% off regular prices before noon
ADDRESS: 1855 W. NW Hwy.
            Grapevine
PHONE: 817-488-5335

FABRIC STORES

CLOTH WORLD

Buy all your sewing needs at Cloth World on Wednesdays, and you'll receive a 10% discount on regularly priced merchandise.

AGE: 55
DISCOUNT: 10%

HANCOCK FABRICS

The complete store for fabrics and sewing supplies is Hancock Fabrics.

AGE: 55
DISCOUNT: 10% first Wednesday of the month

FACTORY STORES AND OUTLET MALLS

Many of the outlet stores contacted are considering organizing a special "senior discount" day, but haven't yet. The centers listed here do offer a senior discount day, and all require you to come by their outlet center office, show your identification with birth date, and they'll issue you a senior discount card to show retailers.

GAINESVILLE FACTORY SHOPS

Bring your checkbook to the Gainesville Factory Shops on Tuesday if you're 55 or better, and get a 10% discount (or more) from the following stores.

ADDRESS: Exit 501 on IH-35
                   Gainesville
PHONE: 817-668-1888

Arthur Treacher's Fish & Chips   BD Baggies
Big & Tall Outlet   Britches
Bruce Alan Bags   Carter's
Casual Corner   Champion Hanes
Chicago Cutlery (15%)   Claire's
Corn Dog 7   Corning Revere*
County Seat   Dansk
Danskin (15%)   Designer Brands Accessories
Easy Spirit   Evan Picone
Factory Brand Shoes   Farah Factory Store*
Farberware   Florsheim
Genuine Kids   Geoffrey Beene*
Gruen (20%)   Guess?
Izod*   Jockey
Jonathan Logan*   Jones New York
Jones New York Woman   Jones New York Executive Style
Kelly Stryker*   Kitchen Collection
Leather Loft   L'eggs Hanes Bali
Levi's Outlet   Maidenform
Naturalizer   Oshkosh B'Gosh
Parkhill's Jewelry   Petite Sophisticate
Prestige Fragrance*   Reebok
Rocky Mountain   S&K Menswear*
Springmaid Wamsutta   Ultra
Van Heusen*   Wallet Works
Welcome Home

SAN MARCOS FACTORY SHOPS

Senior citizens 55+ will receive 10% off at the following San Marcos Factory Shops stores on Tuesdays.

ADDRESS:	3939 IH-35 South
	San Marcos
PHONE:	512-396-2200

* Discount applies to non-sale merchandise only for these stores.

American Tourister

Ashworth

B. D. Baggies

Benetton

Bon Worth

Book Warehouse

Bruce Alan Bags

Capezio

Carole Little

Carter's

Chaus

Chorus Line

Corbin

Colours & Scents

Danskin

Duck Head

Esprit

Famous Brands Housewares

Harry & David

Joan Vass

Jockey

John Henry & Friends

Jonathan Logan

Lammes Candies

Laura Ashley

Leather Loft

London Fog

London Fog Kids

Louis Feraud

Maidenform

Napier

Naturalizer

Nordic Track

Pacific Trail

Paper Factory

Prestige Fragrance & Cosmetics

Pretzel Time

Sharif Collections

So's Hunan

Sony

Stride Rite

Sunglass Outlet

T-Shirts Plus

Teri Jon

Unisa

Villeroy & Boch

SEALY HORIZON OUTLET CENTER

Seniors who are 65 and over will receive a discount at the following stores upon request. They're in the process of organizing a "senior discount day." In addition to these discounts, the management will provide groups of 12 or more with a free discount coupon book and shopping bag when they register at the outlet center office.

ADDRESS: 1402 Outlet Center Drive at I-10
            Sealy

PHONE: 409-835-3200

American Tourister	Specials up to 20% discount
Boardwalk Fries	10% discount every day
Florsheim Shoes	Discounts on selected merchandise
Jockey	10% discount on Tuesdays
Publisher's Warehouse	10% discount on Tuesdays
Savane	10% discount every day
Spiegel	10% discount on Tuesdays

TANGER OUTLET CENTER—SAN MARCOS

Your Silver Tuesday Savings Card will reward you with a 10% discount at these participating Tanger Outlet Stores on Tuesday. This offer is good on regular price merchandise only, and is not valid with other offers or discounts. Please present your card at the point of purchase.

ADDRESS: Exit 200 Center Point Rd.
4015 IH-35 South
San Marcos
PHONE: 512-396-7444

Aileen	American Eagle Outlet
Amity Leather	Big Dog Sportswear
Brown Shoe Co.	Champion Hanes
Chicago Cutlery Etc.	County Seat
Dansk	Farah
Fieldcrest Cannon	Florsheim
**Greetings N' More	Haggar
Izod	Kitchen Collection
L'eggs/Hanes/Bali	Lennox
Levi's	Music For a Song
Pfaltzgraff	*Publisher's Warehouse
Reebok	Royal Doulton
Rue 21	Samsonite
Sara Lee Bakery	Snack Shop
Spiegel Outlet Store	Stone Mountain Handbags
Welcome Home	

* Only good with purchase of $20 or more.
** Only good with purchase of $7.50 or more.

TANGER OUTLET CENTER—TERRELL

Customers who are 55 and better save up to an extra 10% off famous designer and brand name manufacturers every Tuesday at these participating stores. This offer is good on regular priced merchandise only, and is not valid with other offers or discounts. Please present your card at the point of purchase. The center is located 30 minutes from Dallas and 50 minutes from Tyler.

ADDRESS:	I-20 & Hwy. 34
	Terrell
PHONE:	972-524-6255

American Tourister	Big Dog Sportswear
Casual Corner	Corning Revere
Famous Brand Housewares	Farah
Florsheim	John Henry & Friends
Jockey	Kitchen Collection
L'eggs/Hanes/Bali/Playtex	Levi's
Nine West	Paper Factory
Prestige Fragrance	Publisher's Warehouse
Reebok	Rockport
Rocky Mountain Chocolate Factory	S&K Menswear
Vineyard Outlet	Wallet Works
Welcome Home	

FLOWERS, GIFTS, AND JEWELRY

J.R. ABBIE CO.

If you're looking for music boxes, figurines, gifts and collectibles, visit this fine store when you visit Austin's Lakeline Mall. They offer a discount to seniors on the first Tuesday of the month on all regularly priced merchandise, except Armani, Santa's Crystal Valley, and Lilliput Lane products.

AGE:	55
DISCOUNT:	10%
ADDRESS:	11200 Lakeline Mall Dr.
	Lakeline Mall
	Austin
PHONE:	512-257-9528

JAN HAGARA'S DOLL COLLECTIBLES

At Jan Hagara's Doll Collectibles in Georgetown you'll find porcelain dolls and figurines that are collector's items. They also have a large selection of prints, potpourri, plates, and cards. Jan Hagara has a national reputation for finding those limited and almost-sold-out items known as secondary market items, and she'll be happy to have her dealers across the country seek out your dream collectible.

AGE: 60
DISCOUNT: 10% off regularly priced items, except
            porcelain dolls and secondary market items
ADDRESS: 40144 Industrial Park Circle
            Georgetown
PHONE: 512-863-3072

KATHERINE'S FLORAL & GIFTS*

With 20 years of experience, Katherine Stern and Tory Gutierrez can offer florist services, gift baskets, and bridal services for El Paso-area customers. They provide city-wide delivery including Chaparral, New Mexico to Horizon City.

AGE: 55
DISCOUNT: 10%
ADDRESS: 9537 Dyer St.
            El Paso
PHONE: 915-751-9734
FAX: 915-751-9128

Katherine's Floral & Gifts is a member of the Texas Florist Association and can provide fresh floral arrangements for all occasions as well as silk and dried arrangements. They special order exotic flowers from around the world, and church altar arrangements are one of their specialties.

Gift baskets filled with fragrance, fruit, coffee, tea, jam, and jellies created by Katherine's Floral & Gifts have delighted many customers, and these custom-designed baskets are available for shipping.

Katherine's will also help with bridal invitation engraving, hall rental arrangements for military and civilian weddings, tuxedo rentals, and gown rentals and sales, with lay-away plans available. They have a seamstress available and provide wedding consultation at your convenience.

TINA'S BASKETS & FLOWERS

In Austin, call Tina for custom-designed baskets or interior decorator items for your home.

```
AGE:          60
DISCOUNT:     10%
PHONE:        512-926-6948
```

RUSSELL KORMAN JEWELERS

Located just five minutes from the Capitol and The University of Texas at Lamar and 38th Street in Austin, Russell Korman Jewelers is your headquarters for fine jewelry, watches, and silver jewelry. It's no surprise they were selected "Best jewelry store in Austin" by the *Austin Chronicle*.

```
AGE:          55
DISCOUNT:     10% off, except loose diamonds. Mention
              this book, and ask for their "Preferred
              Customer Discount for Texas Seniors."
ADDRESS:      3806 N. Lamar Blvd.
              Austin
PHONE:        512-451-9292
```

Whether you're looking for an impressive selection of diamond engagement rings, estate sale jewelry, anniversary presents, or silver jewelry (great gifts for pre-teens and teens, too), this Austin-owned jewelry store can help you.

---

* (Source: Internet - http://www.bestweb.com/elpaso/referral/kath.htm)

Sports, Fitness, and Personal Care

ASTROS BASEBALL

Watch those Astros bring home the pennant while enjoying a "dome dog" in the Houston Astrodome. Enjoy this senior discount on Sundays when game tickets are purchased at the Dome box office on game day.

AGE: 60
DISCOUNT: $3 off regular prices
PHONE: 713-799-9555

BOWLING

Every bowling center surveyed offers a senior discount on bowling games, but no discount on shoes. Most bowling centers also offer Senior Leagues for bowlers 55 and better. The Texas State Bowling Association also reports there are special bowling awards given to senior bowlers by the American Bowling Congress and the Women's International Bowling Congress.

Please check your telephone directory for a bowling center near you. For more information, call the Texas State Bowling Association at 512-452-1440.

Golf

Municipal Golf Courses

All municipal courses and most of the private golf courses surveyed offer some type of senior discount on green fees and sometimes carts. Expect discounts for seniors 62–65 (ages vary) Monday–Friday, but not necessarily on the weekends. As always, ask about all discounts and also mention you're a senior.

Some of the municipal golf courses have been "privatized" and are being run by private companies with a percentage paid to the city. This arrangement usually results in higher fees for the golfer. Because of this, don't expect the rates at all municipal golf courses to be consistent even within the same city. A sampling of the larger cities surveyed found the following senior programs.

Four of the five Austin municipal courses offer a senior discount with green fees in the $6.50-per-day range. Many of the public golf courses surveyed also offer a senior discount. For information about Austin municipal golf courses, call 512-480-3020.

Dallas municipal courses offer seniors almost a 50% discount off regular fees. Some Dallas public courses offer senior discounts and annual passes with up to 75% discounts. For information about Dallas municipal golf courses, call 214-670-8860.

Houston municipal courses offer a senior discount at six of their seven courses, but the fees vary at each course. For information about Houston municipal golf courses, call 713-772-5674.

San Antonio municipal courses sell a Winter Golf Pass for $40 that gives a discount to golfers vacationing in the area. They also offer a Discount Golf Card (to anyone) with even deeper discounts than their senior citizen discount. The cost is $25 for city residents and $40 for county residents for one year. For information about San Antonio municipal golf courses, call 210-225-3528.

The following gives you an idea of the range of prices for weekday green fees:

Regular Price	Senior Price	Discount Golf Card
$14	$10	$6
$16	$11	$8

Senior Golf Tournaments

There are several golf tournaments and tours in Texas for seniors. Call the phone numbers provided for more information about these events.

Dominion Seniors PGA Tour

Dominion Country Club
San Antonio
210-698-3582

National Super Seniors

Galveston Country Club (for players 65 years and older)
Galveston
409-763-8688

Seniors Golf Tournament

Quail Creek Country Club and Wood Creek Country Club (for players 50 years of age and older)
Seguin and San Marcos
800-580-7322

Senior Women's Golf Championship

Rockport Country Club
Rockport and Fullerton
800-826-6441

The Golf Card*

The Golf Card, offered by Golf Card International, offers seniors and others an international network of over 2,400 golf courses where members enjoy two complimentary rounds of golf per year. The cost is $95 a year for a single membership or $145 for a double membership. Included in the membership is a subscription to *The Golf Traveler* magazine. Changes in the network of affiliated courses are detailed in this magazine. Remember to always call the course first.

PHONE: 800-321-8269

* (Source: *The Golf Card*, The Golf Card, Inc.)

QUEST

If you activate your Golf Card membership card by using it within seven days of receiving it, you'll also receive a free membership to Quest, which gives you the following:

- 50% savings off the regular rates at over 2,000 hotels in the continental U.S., Hawaii, Canada, and Mexico. For example, they say you can save $308 on a four-night stay at the three star Doubletree Suites in Phoenix, Arizona.
- 25% savings at the restaurants in hundreds of those facilities

As an active Golf Card member, simply call any one of their 2,400 courses 24 hours before you want to play, identify yourself as a member of The Golf Card, and arrange for your starting time. You'll pay no green fees the first two times you play on each course. All you pay is the normal fee for a powered golf cart rental. A few courses now charge "player's fees" that include both green fees and cart fees.

Quest includes *selected hotels* from the following chains, plus many more:

Best Western	Days Inn	Clarion
Doubletree	Hilton	Hampton Inn
Holiday Inn	Howard Johnson	Marriott
Omni International	Quality Inn	Radisson
Ramada	Residence Inn	Sheraton
Stouffer	Westin	Wyndham

TEXAS GOLF COURSES

Texas golf courses currently available to The Golf Card Members include the following:

Abilene

Maxwell Municipal Golf Club
915-692-2737

Aledo

Lost Creek Golf Club
817-244-3312

Alice

Alice Country Club
512-664-3723

Alvin

Alvin Golf & Country Club
281-331-4541

Alvin

Hillcrest Golf Club
281-331-3505

Amarillo

Southwest Golf Club
806-355-7161

Atascocita

Atascocita Country Club
281-852-8115

Atlanta

Indian Hills Country Club
903-796-4146

Austin

Riverside Golf Club
512-389-1070

Bandera

Flying L Guest Ranch
800-646-5407

Lost Valley Golf Club
210-460-7958

Bastrop

Lost Pines Golf Club
512-321-2327

Bay City

Rio Colorado Golf Club
409-244-2955

Beeville

John C. Beasley Municipal
Golf Club
512-358-4295

Bowie

Top O' The Lake Country
Club
817-872-5401

Bracketville

Fort Clark Springs Golf Club
210-563-9204

Brady

Brady Municipal Golf Club
915-597-6010

Breckenridge

Breckenridge Country Club
817-559-3466

Bridgeport

Bridgeport Country Club
817-683-9438

Bronte

Singing Winds Golf Club
915-473-2156

Brownfield

Brownfield Country Club
806-637-3656

Brownsville

Brownsville Golf & Recreation
210-541-2582

Fort Brown Golf Club
210-541-0394

Bryan

Bryan Golf Club
409-823-0126

Buchanan Dam

Highland Lakes
   Golf Club
512-793-2859

Burkburnett

River Creek Park Golf Club
817-855-3361

Burnet

Delaware Springs Golf Club
512-756-8471

Caldwell

Coppers Hollow Country Club
409-567-4422

Canadian

Canadian Golf Club
806-323-5512

Canyon

Canyon Country Club
806-499-3397

Palo Duro Creek Golf Club
806-655-1106

Castroville

Alsatian Golf Club
210-931-3100

Canyon Lake

Canyon Lake Golf & Country
   Club
210-899-3372

Cleveland

Cleveland Country Club
281-593-0323

College Station

Greensworld Golf Club
409-764-0596

Colorado City

Wolf Creek Golf Links
915-728-5514

Comanche

P A R Country Club
817-879-2296

Cooper

Delta Country Club
903-395-4712

Copperas Cove

Copperas Cove Municipal
  Golf Club
817-547-2606

Cornith

Oakmont Country Club
817-321-5599

Corpus Christi

Padre Island Country Club
512-949-8006

Corsicana

The Oaks Golf Club
903-872-7252

Cuero

Cuero Municipal Golf Club
512-275-3233

Decatur

Decatur Golf Club
817-627-3789

Denison

Grayson County College
  Golf Club
903-786-9719

Denton

Eagle Point Golf Club
817-387-5180

Devine

Devine Golf Club
210-663-9943

Dimmitt

Country Club of Dimmitt
806-647-4502

Edna

Edna Country Club
512-782-3010

Ennis

The Summit Golf Club
972-878-4653

Falfurrias

Falfurrias Municipal Golf Club
512-325-5348

Farwell

Farwell Country Club
806-481-9210

Flatonia

Flatonia Golf Club
512-865-2922

Frankston

Dogwood Trails Golf Club
903-876-4336

Freeport

Freeport Golf Club
409-233-8311

Frisco

Plantation Golf Club
972-335-4653

Fort Worth

Carswell Golf Club
817-738-8402

Lake Country Club
817-236-3400

Rockwood Golf Club
817-624-1771

Timberview Golf Club
817-478-3601

Galveston

Galveston Island Golf Club
409-744-2366

Ganado

Ganado Golf & Country Club
512-771-2424

Georgetown

Kurth-Landrum Golf Club
512-863-1333

Giddings

Giddings Country Club
409-542-3777

Gladewater

Gladewater Country Club
903-845-4566

Shallow Creek Country Club
903-984-5335

Goldthwaite

Goldthwaite Municipal Golf
  Club
915-938-5652

Goliad

Goliad Golf Club
512-645-8478

Gonzales

Independence Golf Club
210-672-9926

Granbury

Granbury Recreational
817-573-9912

Grand Prairie

Sunset Golf Club
972-331-8057

Groves

Port Groves Golf Club
409-962-4030

Halletsville

Halletsville Golf Club
512-798-9908

Harker Heights

Lakeview Golf & Country Club
817-698-4554

Harlingen

Fairwinds Golf Club
210-423-9433

Hempstead

Hempstead Golf Club
409-826-3212

Henderson

Crepe Myrtle Creek Golf Club
903-657-3325

Henrietta

Clay County Country Club
817-538-4339

Hico

Bluebonnet Country Club
817-796-4122

Hondo

Hondo Golf Club
210-426-2231

Houston

Clear Lake Golf Club
713-738-8000

Idalou

Island Oaks Golf Club
806-892-2839

Jefferson

Rusty Rail Country Club
903-665-7245

Kemp

King's Creek Golf Club
903-498-8888

Kenedy

Karnes County Country Club
210-583-3200

Kermit

Winkler County Golf Club
915-586-9243

Killeen

Killeen Municipal Golf Club
817-699-6034

Kingsland

Packsaddle Country Club
915-388-3863

Kingsville

L. E. Ramey Golf Club
512-592-1101

Kingwood

Kingwood Cove Golf Club
281-358-1155

Lago Vista

Bar-K Public Course
512-267-1226

Highland Lakes Golf Club
512-267-1685

Lago Vista Golf Club
512-267-1179

Lancaster

Lancaster's Country View
  Golf Club
972-227-0995

Leander

Crystal Falls Golf Club
512-259-5855

Point Venture Country Club
512-267-1151

Lewisville

Lake Park Golf Club
972-436-5332

Littlefield

Littlefield Golf Club
806-385-3309

Livingston

Mill Ridge Golf Club
409-327-3535

Llano

Llano Golf Club
915-247-5100

Lockhart

Lockhart State Park Golf Club
512-398-3479

Longview

Alpine Golf Club
903-753-4515

Longview Country Club
903-759-9251

Wood Hollow Golf Club
903-663-4653

Lubbock

Elm Grove Country Club
806-799-7801

Pine Valley Golf Club
806-748-1448

Shadow Hills Golf Club
806-793-9700

Madisonville

Oak Ridge Country Club
409-348-6264

Marble Falls

Blue Lake Golf Club
210-598-5524

Meadowlakes Golf &
  Country Club
210-693-3300

Mart

Battle Lake Golf Club
817-876-2837

McKinney

Hank Haney Golf Ranch
972-542-8800

Mercedes

Llano Grande Golf Club
210-565-3351

Merkel

Merkel Country Club
915-928-3193

Mexia

Olde Oaks Golf &
Country Club
817-562-2391

Mission

Seven Oaks Resort &
Country Club
210-581-6267

Morton

Morton Country Club
806-266-5941

Muleshoe

Muleshoe Country Club
806-272-4250

Murchison

Echo Creek Country Club
903-852-7094

Nacogdoches

Woodland Hills Golf Club
409-564-2762

Navasota

Bluebonnet Country Club
409-894-2207

Nocona

Nocona Golf Club
817-825-4213

Nocona Hills Country Club
817-825-3444

Olton

Olton Country Club
806-285-2595

Palacios

Palacios Golf Club
512-972-2666

Pampa

Hidden Hills Public Golf Club
806-669-5866

Paris

Elk Hollow Golf Club
903-785-6585

Pine Ridge Golf Club
903-785-8076

Pflugerville

Blackhawk Golf Club
512-251-9000

Plano

Los Rios Country Club
972-424-8913

Post

Caprock Golf Club
806-495-3029

Refugio

Refugio County Country Club
512-526-9188

Rising Star

Lakewood Recreation Center
817-643-7792

Robert Lee

Mountain Creek Golf Club
915-453-2317

Round Rock

Forest Creek Golf Club
512-388-2874

Rusk

Birmingham Golf Club
903-683-9518

Sam Rayburn

Rayburn Country Resort &
   Country Club
409-698-2958

San Antonio

Pecan Valley Golf Club
210-333-9018

Woodlake Country Club
210-661-6124

San Marcos

Aquarena Springs Resort
512-392-2710

San Saba

San Saba Golf Club
915-372-3212

Seguin

Chaparral Country Club
210-303-0669

Shamrock

Shamrock Country Club
806-256-5151

Sherman

Woodlawn Country Club
903-893-3240

Slaton

Slaton Municipal Golf Club
806-828-3269

Spicewood

Pedernales Golf Club
512-264-1489

Sulphur Springs

Sulphur Springs Country Club
903-885-4861

Sundown

Sundown Municipal Golf Club
806-229-6186

Sweetwater

Lake Sweetwater Golf Club
915-235-8816

Taylor

Mustang Creek Golf Club
512-365-1332

Teague

Freestone Country Club
817-739-3272

Temple

Sammons Golf Club
817-778-8282

Texas City

Trinity Plantation
   Country Club
409-643-5850

Trinity

Trinity Plantation
   Country Club
409-594-2583

Tulia

Tule Lake Golf Club
806-995-3400

Tyler

Cross Creek Golf Club
903-597-4871

Victoria

Colony Creek Country Club
512-576-0020

Waco

Better Golf, Inc.
817-848-4831

Bogey's Golf Club
817-754-4401

James Connally Golf Club
817-799-6561

Western Oaks Country Club
817-772-8100

Weatherford

Horseshoe Bend Country Club
817-594-6454

Live Oak Country Club
817-594-7596

Weimar

Hill Memorial Park Golf Club
409-725-8624

Whitney

Lake Whitney Golf Club
817-694-2313

Wichita Falls

Weeks Park Golf Club
817-767-6107

Wimberley

Woodcreek Resort
512-847-9700

Winters

Winters Country Club
915-754-4679

Woodville

Dogwood Hills Country Club
409-283-8725

Yoakum

Yoakum Municipal Golf Club
512-293-5682

RACING

If you're a fan of greyhound, quarter horse, or thoroughbred racing, you'll find it in Texas. The Texas Racing Commission has two greyhound racetracks and four horse racetracks licensed and operational. For specific details on each track, visit the Texas Racing Commission's web site. On their site, you will also find current year race dates, statistical information about Texas racing, glossary of racing terms, and wagering information and terminology.

PHONE: 512-833-6699
INTERNET: http://txrc6.txrc.state.tx.us/tracks.html

CORPUS CHRISTI GREYHOUND RACETRACK

Admission to the track is free to seniors 60 and older for Wednesday, Saturday, and Sunday matinees. Gates open at noon at this six-year-old track, and matinees are generally 1:30 p.m. to 4:30 p.m. This racetrack is located just off Interstate 37 in Corpus Christi.

AGE: 60
ADDRESS: 5302 Leopart St.
           Corpus Christi
PHONE: 800-580-7223

GULF GREYHOUND PARK

Spend a free afternoon betting on your favorite greyhound in La Marque. Seniors get in free on Wednesdays beginning at 4 p.m. and Fridays beginning at 1:30 p.m.

AGE: 62
COST: Free
ADDRESS: 1000 FM 2004
           La Marque
PHONE: 800-ASK-2WIN (800-275-2946)
INTERNET: http://www.gulfgreyhound.com

LONE STAR PARK AT GRAND PRAIRIE

This track opened for business May 3, 1996. Patrons can enjoy seating in their 280,000-square-foot glass-enclosed, climate-controlled grandstand. Special seating and other benefits are available through membership in their Jockey Club, Homestretch Boxes, and Finish Line Boxes programs. They offer a special senior package during their Fall Meeting of Champions Race Event held in October. For $8.50, seniors 65 and over receive admission, program, reserved parking, and seating. All they have to do is pick the winners! The Lone Star Park schedules both thoroughbred and quarter horse races. You'll find this track located in the middle of the Dallas/Fort Worth metroplex in Grand Prairie on Belt Line Road north of Interstate 30.

PHONE: 972-263-7223
ADDRESS: 1001 Meyers Rd.
           Grand Prairie
INTERNET: http://www.lonestarpark.com

Manor Downs

Manor Downs is located approximately 10 miles east of Austin. This track has been open for 20 years, and has free parking. Seniors enter free Wednesdays through Fridays, with parking for $1. Manor Downs offers simulcast races Wednesdays through Sundays and live races on Saturdays and Sundays, March 1 through June 8.

AGE: 60
ADDRESS: 101 Hill Lane
              Manor
PHONE: 512-272-5581

Retama Park

They're OFF! At Retama Park, 15 miles north of San Antonio, you'll enjoy daily, year-round horse racing. Admission for active duty and retired military is free, and general parking is $1.

AGE: 62
DISCOUNT: $1 off in General Area and Clubhouse
PHONE: 210-651-7000

Sam Houston Race Park

This racetrack is located in northwest Houston just south of Beltway 8 between Highway 290 and Interstate 45. They offer live racing Thursdays through Sundays, with simulcasting 364 days a year.

AGE: 62
DISCOUNT: $2 off ($1 for seniors in groups of 10 or
              more Wednesday through Friday nights)
ADDRESS: 7777 N. Sam Houston Pkwy.
              Houston
INTERNET: http://www.shrp.com

TENNIS

A survey of tennis organizations around the state found that most of them offer a senior discount on games. Many private clubs offer a discount for senior membership and offer senior tournaments. Many of the tennis centers listed offer a senior discount, but some may not. The following is a list of Texas tennis facilities provided by the Texas Tennis Association.

TEXAS TENNIS FACILITIES

Abilene

Abilene Country Club
4039 S. Treadway
915-695-6712

Rose Park Tennis Center
810 Portland
915-673-8396

Amarillo

Amarillo Country Club
4800 Bushland
806-355-5687

Amarillo Tennis Center
2501 Elmwood
806-378-4213

Tascosa Country Club
2400 Western St.
806-376-4771

Amarillo Town Club
4514 Cornell
806-355-9636

Arlington

Rolling Hills Country Club
401 Lamar Blvd. West
972-274-1072

Austin

Austin Country Club
4408 Long Champ Dr.
512-326-0090

Austin Recreation Center
12th St. at Shoal Creek
512-476-5662

Balcones Country Club
11210 Spicewood Club Ln.
512-258-6672

Barton Creek Country Club
3101 Exposition
512-329-4000

Caswell Tennis Club
2312 Shoal Creek
512-473-6268

Courtyard Tennis & Swim Club
5608 Courtyard Dr.
512-345-4700

Lakeway World of Tennis
One World of Tennis Sq.
512-261-7222

Lost Creek Country Club
1 Lost Creek Dr.
512-892-0173

Onion Creek Country Club
2510 Onion Creek Pkwy.
512-282-2829

Pharr Tennis Club
4201 Brookview
512-477-7773

South Austin Tennis Center
Cumberland at S. 5th St.
512-442-1466

Westover Hills Club
8706 Westover Club Dr.
512-346-9497

Carrollton

Columbian Country Club
2525 Country Club Dr.
972-416-2187

Country Place
2727 Country Place Dr.
972-245-4200

Corpus Christi

Al Kruse Tennis Club
502 King St.
512-883-6342

Corpus Christi Athletic Club
2101 Airline Rd.
512-992-7100

Corpus Christi Country Club
6300 Everhart
512-991-7561

H.E.B. Tennis Club
1520 W. Shely
512-882-6013

Kings Crossing Golf &
   Country Club
6201 OSO Pkwy.
512-991-2582

Pharoah Country Club
7111 Pharoah Dr.
512-991-6604

DFW Airport

Bear Creek Golf &
   Racquet Club
DFW Airport
817-615-6808

Dallas

Aerobics Center
12100 Preston Rd.
972-233-4832

Bent Tree Country Club
5201 Westgrove
972-931-7326

Brookhaven Country Club
3334 Golfing Green Dr.
972-241-5961

Brookhollow Country Club
8301 Harry Hines
214-637-4440

Dallas Country Club
4155 Beverly Dr.
214-521-1820

Fair Oaks Tennis Club
7501 Merriean Pkwy.
214-670-1495

Fretz Tennis Club
14700 Hillcrest
214-670-6622

Kiest Tennis Club
2324 W. Kiest Blvd.
214-670-7616

L. B. Houston Tennis Club
11223 Luna Rd.
214-670-6367

Lakewood Country Club
6430 Gaston Ave.
214-821-8440

Northwood Club
6524 Alpha Rd.
972-239-3402

Oak Cliff Country Club
2200 W. Red Bird Ln.
214-333-2197

Prestonwood Country Club
15909 Preston Rd.
972-239-1935

Royal Oaks Country Club
7915 Greenville Ave.
214-691-3313

Samuel Grand Tennis Club
6200 E Grand Ave.
214-670-1374

Seay Tennis Club
7015 Westchester
214-521-2745

T-Bar-M Racquet Club
6060 Dilbeck
972-233-4444

University Club of Dallas
13350 Dallas Pkwy.
972-239-0051

Verandah Club
2201 Stemmons
214-761-7878

Village Tennis Club
8310 Southwestern Blvd.
214-363-3471

Denton

Goldfield Tennis Club
321 E. McKinney
817-566-8485

Desoto

Thorntree Country Club
825 W. Wintergreen
972-298-0017

Euless

Sotogrande Tennis Club
3601 Pipeline Rd. North
817-283-6611

Fort Worth

Colonial Country Club
3735 CC Circle
817-927-6250

Dan Danciger Jewish
  Community Center
6801 Old Granbury Rd.
817-292-3111

Diamond Oaks Country Club
5821 Diamond Oaks Dr.
817-834-6261

Eastchase Racquet Club
9055 John T. White Rd.
817-469-9505

General Dynamics Recreation
4800 Bryant Irving Rd.
817-732-1761

Mary Potishean Lard
  Tennis Club
3609 Bellaire Dr. North
817-921-7960

McLeland Tennis Club
1600 W. Seminary Dr.
817-921-5134

Mira Vista Country Club
6600 Mira Vista Blvd.
817-294-6600

Ridglea Country Club
3700 Bernie Anderson
817-732-3174

River Crest Country Club
1501 Western Ave.
817-738-9221

Shady Oaks Country Club
320 Roaring Springs Rd.
817-732-3303

Woodhaven Country Club
913 Country Club Ln.
817-457-5160

Frisco

Stonebriar Country Club
5050 Country Club Dr.
281-625-9276

Garland

Oak Ridge Country Club
2800 Diamond Oak Dr.
972-530-8020

Spring Park Health &
  Racquet Club
3330 Spring Park Way
972-495-5552

Eastern Hills Country Club
3000 Country Club Rd.
972-271-4876

Garland Tennis Center
1010 Miller Rd.
972-205-2778

The Trails Tennis &
Swim Club
725 Trails Pkwy.
972-279-6863

Georgetown

Berry Creek Country Club
409 Serenada
512-903-3783

Granbury

Hill Top Tennis Club
1 Thistle Ridge Rd.
817-326-5566

Grand Prairie

Woodcrest Country Club
3502 Country Club Dr.
972-263-6674

Grapevine

DFW Airport Hilton
1800 Hwy. 26 East
972-481-8444

Hereford

Hereford Country Club
726 Country Club Dr.
806-364-3411

Houston

Bay Area Racquet Club
17901 Kings Park Ln.
281-488-7025

Briar Club
2603 Timmons Ln.
713-622-2667

Dad's Club YMCA
1006 Voss Rd.
713-467-5911

Fondren Tennis Club
3035 Crossview
713-784-4010

Full Court Volley at Oakwood
7512 Burgoyne
713-977-1915

Greenwood Forest Resort Club
12700 Champion Forest
281-444-3522

Houston Country Club
1 Potomac Dr.
713-465-0367

Houston City Club
9 Greenway Plaza
713-840-0255

Houston Indoor Tennis Club
945 Bunker Hill
713-467-7770

Houstonian Club
111 N. Post Oak Ln.
713-680-3330

Lakeside Country Club
100 Wilcrest
281-497-2229

Memorial Park Tennis Club
1500 Memorial Loop
713-861-3765

Metropolitan Racquet Club
1 Allen Ctr.
713-652-0700

Northgate Country Club
17110 Northgate Forest Dr.
281-440-1224

Olde Oaks Tennis Club
14647 Walters Rd.
281-444-6750

Post Oak YMCA
1331 Augusta Dr.
713-781-1061

Steeplechase Swim & Racquet
11250 Steepleway
281-890-6878

Tennis World Racquet Club
11201 Olympia
713-785-0992

The Forest Club
9550 Memorial Dr.
713-686-3720

University Club
5501 Westheimer
713-622-5921

Westside Tennis Club
1200 Wilcrest
713-783-1620

Westwood Country Club
8888 Country Creek
713-774-2571

Windmere Racquet &
   Swim Club
123 Lakeside Ln.
281-333-5163

Irving

Eldorado Country Club
2604 Country Club Dr.
972-952-9762

Hackburry Country Club
1901 Royal Ln.
972-869-1503

Las Colinas Country Club
4900 N. O'Connor Blvd.
972-541-1141

Las Colinas Sports Club
4200 N. McArthur Blvd.
972-717-2540

Stonebridge Country Club
7003 Beaton Hill Rd.
972-540-1000

Longview

Oak Forest Country Club
601 Thomelson Pkwy.
972-297-3932

Lubbock

Lakeridge Country Club
8802 Vicksburg
806-794-4444

Lubbock Municipal
   Tennis Center
3060 66th St.
806-752-0743

Lubbock Racquet &
   Athletic Club
9000 Memphis Dr.
806-795-0675

Lufkin

Crown Colony Country Club
900 Crown Colony Dr.
214-634-4927

Live Well Athletic Club
1616 Tulane
409-639-LIVE

Mansfield

Walnut Creek Country Club
1151 Country Club Dr.
817-473-1311

Marble Falls

Meadowlakes
2020 Meadowlakes Dr.
512-693-7826

McAllen

McAllen Country Club
615 Wichita
210-682-3459

Midland

Boys Club of Midland
1110 E. New Jersey
915-683-5297

Greentree Country Club
4900 Green Tree Blvd.
915-697-7806

Midland Country Club
Rt. 12
915-682-4376

Midland Parks & Recreation
  Department
300 Baldwin
915-683-4291

Ranchland Hills Country Club
1600 E. Wadley
915-682-4104

The Midlander
Corporate Dr.
915-632-0513

Mineral Wells

Holiday Hills Country Club
Weatherford Hwy.
817-325-9442

Mission

The Club at Cimmeron
1200 S. Shary Rd.
210-581-7405

New Braunfels

John Newcombe's
  Tennis Ranch
Hwy. 46 at Mission Valley Rd.
210-625-9105

Odessa

Mission Dorado Country Club
1 Mission Blvd.
915-563-4707

Odessa Country Club
East Hwy. 80
915-362-0001

Perryton

The Perryton Club
520 SE 24th Ave.
806-435-6523

Plano

Bieneagles Country Club
5401 W. Park Blvd.
972-867-6666

Country Place
3600 Country Place Dr.
972-985-8855

High Point Tennis Center
421 Spring Creek Pkwy.
972-578-7170

Los Rios Country Club
1700 Country Club Dr.
972-423-1700

Willowbend Tennis Club
5845 W. Park Blvd.
972-248-6298

Richardson

Canyon Creek Country Club
625 Lookout Dr.
972-231-2881

Hoffheines Tennis Center
3106 Bluestem
972-234-6697

Roanoke

Trophy Club Country Club
500 Trophy Club Dr.
214-430-0059

Rockport

Rockport Country Club
101 Champions Dr.
512-729-8324

Rockwall

Chardier's Landing
   Racquet Club
501 Yacht Club Dr. South
972-771-2051

The Shores Country Club
2600 Champions Dr.
972-771-0302

San Angelo

Bentwood Country Club
2111 Clubhouse Ln.
915-949-1534

Southland Swim &
   Racquet Club
2500 Greenbriar Ln.
915-949-5094

Sherman

Four Seasons Tennis Club
Hwy. 1417 North
972-868-9572

Temple

Racquet Club of Temple
620 Fryers Creek Circle South
817-773-2121

Wildflower Country Club
4902 Wildflower Ln.
817-771-1177

Terrell

Terrell Tennis Club
530 Samuels Rd.
972-563-6543

Tyler

Holly Tree Country Club
6700 Hollytree Dr.
903-581-7788

Tyler Tennis & Swim Club
320 Shiloh Rd.
972-561-3014

Vernon

Hillcrest Country Club
Hillcrest Dr.
817-552-5406

Waco

Charlie McCleary Tennis Club
1301 Barnard
817-756-0371

Lakewood Tennis &
   Country Club
4005 Lake Shore Dr.
817-753-7441

Ridgewood Country Club
7100 Rish Pond Rd.
817-772-0991

Weatherford

City of Weatherford
Recreation Department
817-594-5441

Westlake

The Solana Club
2902 Sans School Rd.
817-491-4553

Whitney

Lake Whitney Country Club
FM 933 West
817-477-3582

Wichita Falls

Hamilton Park Tennis Club
2101 Hamilton
817-766-2321

Jody Ann White School
   of Tennis
4203 Seabury Dr.
817-696-1420

Weeks Park Tennis Club
4101 Weeks Park Ln.
817-322-6600

Wichita Falls Country Club
1701 Hamilton Blvd.
817-767-6321

FITNESS

BODYBUSINESS HEALTH & FITNESS CLUB

BodyBusiness has been an Austin-owned and operated full-service fitness facility since 1984. They have designed several of their programs with seniors in mind. In addition, one of their club membership plans for seniors allows a discount for Seton Good Health Club 65+ members (see Chapter 10, Medical and Dental Services, for details).

```
AGE:          60
DISCOUNT:     Waive initial fee (call for details)
ADDRESS:      2700 W. Anderson Ln.
              The Village Shopping Center
              Austin
PHONE:        512-459-9424
```

Diamond Members 60+ Full Facility Membership allows unlimited access to the BodyBusiness facility including the indoor heated pool, whirlpool, weight room, and senior fitness classes. It includes extensive aqua aerobic classes and the arthritis aqua exercise classes taught by Arthritis Foundation certified instructors. There are special rates for couples.

STUDIO ONE

Enjoy this Seniorcise Exercise program of gentle, but challenging movement sponsored by the Austin Parks and Recreation Department. You can also enjoy lunch for a $1 donation.

```
AGE:          50
COST:         $5 per year
ADDRESS:      3911 Manchaca
              Austin
PHONE:        512-338-1599
```

YMCA OF THE USA

Check out your local YMCA when you're looking for fitness programs. There are 82 YMCAs in Texas. Because they are individually owned and managed, expect to find varying membership fees, facilities, and programs offered across the state. It is possible to participate in individual programs without buying a membership to the YMCA. Some, but not all, YMCAs participate in the "Away" program. This allows you a specified number of free visits at another participating YMCA when you're traveling.

PHONE: 800-872-9622

These are the senior programs offered at participating YMCA locations in Texas:

- Senior Fitness/Exercise
- Senior Adult Instructional Classes
- Senior Trips and Programs
- Senior Social Clubs
- Senior Citizen Center
- Senior Sports League
- Senior Strength Training

PERSONAL CARE

BEAUTY COLLEGES

Many large Texas cities have a beauty school where supervised students provide cosmetology services. These colleges are licensed by the Texas Cosmetology Commission, and the Commission will provide a list of all these facilities for $35. The services provided at each college vary, but generally include all hair care services, manicures, and pedicures, sculptured nails, and facials.

CENTRAL TEXAS BEAUTY COLLEGE

This school for budding hair stylists offers discounts for seniors all day Tuesday–Friday on haircuts (including shampoo) and permanents. All of their services are performed by supervised students.

AGE: 62
DISCOUNT: $1 off standard prices (Tuesday through Friday 10 a.m.–6 p.m.)
ADDRESS: 1208 N. IH-35
North Village Shopping Center
Round Rock
PHONE: 512-206-0525

VOGUE BEAUTY COLLEGE

Vogue Beauty Colleges provide all hair care services including cut, color, set, and permanents. They also provide sculptured nails, manicures, and pedicures, facials, and facial waxing. There are Vogue Beauty Colleges in 11 Texas cities. Please consult the Index in the back of the book to find out if one is located near you.

ELAINE BOND

Elaine specializes in color and perms and often cuts and styles hair in Austin-area senior centers. Call her salon to schedule an appointment.

COST: $15 shampoo, cut, and style, Tuesdays and Thursdays
PHONE: 512-328-2097 or 512-312-1634

C&S BARBER & BEAUTY SALON

For discounts on hair cuts, permanents, and Matrix product hair color, visit this Austin beauty salon. You may call for an appointment or just come by.

AGE: 60
DISCOUNT: 10% off Monday-Friday, before noon
ADDRESS: 5725 N. IH-35
                 Austin
PHONE: 512-451-2534

SUPERCUTS

Supercuts will give you a quick professional cut with shampooing and blow drying for an extra charge. They also sell hair supplies. Most salons will let you call and put your name on the waiting list on week days; otherwise, it's first come first served.

AGE: 55
DISCOUNT: $2

Tours

Blue Bell Ice Cream Tour

See if Brenham really is heaven when you sample ice cream on the Blue Bell Creamery tour. Be sure to call in advance to check their tour schedule—they say it varies a lot. Groups should plan to make reservations at least two weeks in advance. The tour will take about 45 minutes and is wheelchair accessible.

AGE: 55
COST: $1.50 for seniors
PHONE: 800-327-8135

Capitol Tour

On your visit to Austin, stop and see the newly restored state Capitol and underground extension. Call 512-463-0063 to verify the schedule. The free tour takes about an hour and is usually scheduled:

Monday–Friday 8:30 a.m. to 4:30 p.m.
Saturday 9:30 a.m. to 4:30 p.m.
Sunday 12:30 p.m. to 4:30 p.m.

There are also guided walking tours and free brochures at 201 E. Second St. Call the Austin Visitors and Convention Bureau at 800-926-2282 and listen to their recording of upcoming events and tours. They'll also mail you a visitors packet if you ask.

GOVERNOR'S MANSION TOUR

Tour the Governor's Mansion when you're in Austin. It's free, just be sure to call and verify the tour schedule and make reservations for groups. The usual schedule is Monday through Friday, every 20 minutes between 10 a.m. and 11:40 a.m. When other activities occur at the mansion, the tour schedule may be interrupted. (Refer to Chapter 6, Free Stuff and Other Senior Discounts, for more information about the governor.) You'll begin the tour at 1010 Colorado.

AGE: Any age
COST: Free
PHONE: 512-463-5516 (up-to-the-minute
            Governor's Mansion closing schedule)

HUMMEL MUSEUM

New Braunfels is the home of the world's largest collection of original Hummel art open to the public. There are hundreds of priceless figurines, over 354 paintings and drawings, and a 30-minute video showing how the figures are created.

AGE: 65
DISCOUNT: 50 cents ($4.50 for seniors)

NATIONAL WILDFLOWER RESEARCH CENTER*

Take a relaxing stroll through 23 colorful display gardens and enjoy some cappuccino or lunch at the Wildflower Cafe. Or, browse through the Wild Ideas gift store or Research Library. I'm sure Lady Bird Johnson feels there's no better place in Texas to stop and "smell the roses." They're open year-round, but closed on Mondays and major holidays. Call

---

* (Source: *National Wildflower Research Center General Information*, National Wildflower Research Center)

the Registrar's Office for group rates or to make reservations for guided tours.

AGE: 60
DISCOUNT: $1.50 off ($2 for students and seniors)
ADDRESS: 4801 La Crosse Ave.
              Austin
PHONE: 512-292-4100

NATURAL BRIDGE CAVERNS

When you need to beat the Texas heat, visit this 60-foot natural limestone bridge that remains a comfortable 70 degrees year-round. It is 140 million years old and still growing!

AGE: 65
DISCOUNT: 75 cents off ($6.25 for seniors)
ADDRESS: 26495 Natural Bridge Caverns Rd.
              San Antonio
PHONE: 210-651-6101

SPACE CENTER HOUSTON*

Space Center Houston will take you on a journey into the past, present, and future of NASA's manned space flight program.

AGE: 50
DISCOUNT: 10% off
COST: $10.75 for seniors
PHONE: 800-972-0369

The facility is wheelchair accessible, and wheelchairs can be rented at the front gate. You can eat at the Zero-G Diner and shop for souvenirs in the Space Trader Gift Shop. There's an air conditioned kennel for the pets, but remember to bring Fido's own water dish.

---

* (Source: *A Magical Place to Discover Space*, Space Center Houston)

Texas State Aquarium*

Have a "near-ocean" experience when you visit the Texas State Aquarium. It's right at the center of Corpus Christi's bay front, and nearby you'll find the USS Lexington, the Corpus Christi Museum of Science & History, the Art Museum of South Texas, the Watergarden, and the Harbor Playhouse.

AGE: 55
DISCOUNT: 27% ($5.75 for seniors)
PHONE: 800-477-GULF (800-477-4853)

USS Lexington Museum on the Bay**

One of the most famous aircraft carriers in the history of the U.S. Navy is permanently docked in Corpus Christi and is ready for inspection! You'll relive its history through multimedia exhibits like "Kamikaze" and historic planes that include a Blue Angels jet and an F-14, the Top Gun of Navy aircraft. The USS Lexington is located next to the Texas State Aquarium on Corpus Christi Beach.

AGE: 60
DISCOUNT: $2
COST: $6 for seniors
PHONE: 800-LADY LEX (800-523-9539)

---

 * (Source: *A Whole New SEAson,* Corpus Christi Texas State Aquarium)
** (Source: *LEX!,* USS Lexington)

Index by Cities

NationsBank, 20
Ramada, 80
Sears, 148
Supercuts, 193
Texas State Optical (TSO), 113
U-Haul Co., 9
Weeks Park Golf Club, 178
Weeks Park Tennis Club, 189
Wichita Falls Convention &
    Visitors Bureau, 66
Wichita Falls Country Club, 189
YMCA, 191

Willis
U-Haul Co., 9

Wills Point
Lake Tawakoni State Park, 43

Wimberley
U-Haul Co., 9
Woodcreek Resort, 178

Windcrest
Michaels Arts and Crafts, 157
Shoney's Restaurant, 129

Winnie
Waffle House, 132

Winnsboro
U-Haul Co., 9

Winters
U-Haul Co., 9
Winters Country Club, 178

Wolfe City
U-Haul Co., 9

Woodville
Dogwood Hills Country
    Club, 178

Wylie
U-Haul Co., 9

Yoakum
U-Haul Co., 9
Yoakum Municipal Golf
    Club, 178

Yorktown
U-Haul Co., 9

Zapata
Falcon State Park, 43

Zavalla
Angelina National Forest, 28

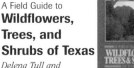